THE COUNTRY MOUSE

A Cookbook for Cheese Lovers

THE COUNTRY MOUSE

A Cookbook for Cheese Lovers

by Sally Walton
and Faye Wilkinson

Illustrated by Tupper Davidson

QUAIL RIDGE PRESS

*Lovingly dedicated
to our cheese-loving families
Harry and Herb
Mimi and Philip
Bert and Brad*

Copyright © 1983 by
QUAIL RIDGE PRESS, INC.
First printing, July 1983
Second printing, July 1984
ISBN 0-937552-10-0
Manufactured in the United States of America
Designed and edited by Gwen McKee

CONTENTS

Preface/Acknowledgment 6
The Country Mouse Visits the City Mouse 7
   (Microwave, breakfasts, salads, quick dishes)
The Country Mouse in Her Country House 21
   (Farm-fresh vegetables, eggs, casseroles)
The Country Mouse Has a Wine and Cheese Party 31
   (Hors d'oeuvres, logs, dips, spreads, desserts)
The Country Mouse Takes a Trip 41
   (Mexican, Greek, Italian, German, French dishes)
The Country Mouse Goes to the Church Bazaar 51
   (Breads, cakes, desserts)
The Country Mouse Has a Dinner Party 61
   (Salads, soups, vegetables, meats, desserts)
Cheese Facts 74
Index 77

PREFACE/ACKNOWLEDGMENT

The Country Mouse is actually "two mice" who live in Vicksburg, Mississippi, and who share a special fondness for cheese. "Sally Mouse" owes much of her cheese education to the experience of working in a cheese shop. And "Faye Mouse," who is a school teacher, owes hers to the enjoyment of entertaining with cheese dishes in her home.

This book is intended to be a fun way of sharing with other cheese lovers our favorite recipes and experiences in using and cooking with cheese.

We warmly acknowledge our good friends who shared their favorite recipes with us and tested many more: Phyllis, Martha, Pat, Peggy E., Joyce, Denise, Carolyn, Tupper, Mary, Peggy G., Carol, Larraine, Beth, Marion, Abby, Nancy, Judy, Marilyn, and Belinda.

We also wish to thank our close friend, Tupper, whose illustrations are absolutely delightful and whose enthusiam was always contagious.

Sally Walton and Faye Wilkinson

THE CHEESE BOARD

The Country Mouse Visits the City Mouse

*From nine to five she works at her job
Yet turns out a meal with nary a sob.*

*Her specialties are breakfast—nutritious and quick
And lunches that a working Mom would pick.*

*The City Mouse uses a microwave,
Her family to please, her time to save!*

COLONIAL BREAKFAST

Cottage cheese
Jam or jelly

Breakfast breads, toast, rolls,
or biscuits

As the early settlers of New England did each morning, use cottage cheese as a spread for breakfast breads, toast, rolls, or biscuits and top it with your favorite jams or jellies.

BAGEL BREAKFAST TREAT

Bagels, sliced and toasted
Cream cheese and chives

Smoked salmon or sliced
tomatoes

Spread cream cheese with chives on toasted bagels. Cover with slices of smoked salmon and/or slices of tomatoes. Or try toasted bagels with smoked process cheese.

EGGS GRUYERE FOR TWO

2 (1-ounce) packages
Gruyere cheese

1 English muffin, halved
2 eggs, poached

Spread a process Gruyere cheese triangle on the halves of an untoasted English muffin. While allowing the Gruyere to melt under the broiler, poach 2 eggs. When cooked, place the hot eggs on the English muffin halves and serve.

COFFEE LOVER'S OMELETTE

Cook an omelette on one side until solidified. Spread a spoonful of currant jelly on the open side, fold in half and top with sharp Cheddar cheese. Bake in moderate oven 5 minutes or till cheese melts. The Cheddar/currant combination is most pleasing.

BEE MY HONEY FRENCH TOAST

Spread hot French toast with cream cheese instead of butter for a tasty variation of a fine old standard. Top with honey or jam. Or try the same with pancakes or waffles.

GOUDA EGGS

Scramble eggs. Season with salt and pepper, if desired. Add about 1 tablespoon shredded Gouda (or a spoonful of a cheese spread, some softened cream cheese or some shredded Cheddar) to the eggs during the last few minutes of cooking. When the cheese has melted, the dish is ready to serve.

BREAKFAST SAUSAGE APPLE PIE

16 ounces pork sausage links
1 (11-ounce) package pie crust mix or make your own
1 (20-ounce) can apple pie filling
1 cup (4 ounces) shredded Cheddar cheese
½ cup firmly packed light brown sugar

Cook sausage links well in large skillet; drain on paper towels. Prepare pie shell with half of pie crust mix; prick with fork; bake in 375-degree oven 10 minutes. Spoon pie filling into partially baked shell; arrange cooked sausage spoke fashion on filling; sprinkle with shredded cheese.

Combine remaining half of pie crust mix with brown sugar in a small bowl; sprinkle over top of pie. Bake an additional 25 minutes or until crust is golden brown. Warm and hearty.

SUNRISE SURPRISE

1 English muffin, halved
Mayonnaise
1 slice Swiss cheese
1 slice cooked ham or Canadian bacon
1 slice pineapple

To begin your day with extra energy, split an English muffin and spread it with mayonnaise. Place a slice of a Swiss-type cheese on each half, adding next a slice of cooked ham or Canadian bacon, and top the whole thing with a round of pineapple. (Pretty to add a Maraschino cherry in center of pineapple for color.) Broil until the cheese has melted and the pineapple is warm.

SPEEDY MICRO BREAKFAST

1½ slices boiled ham
1 egg
Salt and pepper to taste
2 tablespoons grated Cheddar cheese
Nutmeg

Grease a small custard cup. Cut ham into pieces to fit sides and bottom of cup. Break egg onto ham in cup. Prick yolk with the tip of a knife; season with salt and pepper. Sprinkle with grated cheese. Add a dash of nutmeg. Cover tightly with plastic wrap. Microwave 1½ minutes on Medium High. Let stand, covered, 1-3 minutes, to desired degree of doneness. Serve with toast.

EGGS PARMIGIANA

Fry or scramble eggs and sprinkle salt, pepper and a bit of fresh grated Parmesan cheese on top of eggs immediately before removing from pan. Easy and good!

RAINBOW SALAD

Slice a fresh orange and a ripe banana; add a handful of seedless grapes, some berries in season, and a diced avocado. Toss lightly and arrange in the center of a serving plate. Surround with a ring of creamed cottage or Ricotta cheese.

RED RIVER MOUNTAIN SALAD

For each serving, mound about 1/3 cup Ricotta cheese onto crisp lettuce. Make an indention in the top of each mound and spoon about 2 tablespoons of cranberry-orange relish into it, allowing some to drip over the sides of the white "mountain." Top with chopped pistachio nuts and surround with mandarin orange sections. Pretty.

PINK ARCTIC FREEZE

2 (3-ounce) packages cream cheese
2 tablespoons mayonnaise
2 tablespoons sugar
½ cup chopped walnuts
1 (16-ounce can whole cranberry sauce)
1 (9-ounce) can pineapple tidbits, drained
1 cup heavy cream, whipped

Soften cheese; blend in mayonnaise and sugar. Add nuts and fruit. Fold in whipped cream. Pour into loaf pan. Freeze firm 6 hours or overnight. To serve, let stand at room temperature about 15 minutes. Turn out on a bed of lettuce; slice. For luncheon, serve with dainty chicken or ham sandwiches or serve with cookies for a dessert. Serves 8-10.

FRUIT SALAD WITH CREAM CHEESE PEARLS

Make your favorite fruit salad using seasonal fruits. Instead of a dressing, garnish with softened cream or Neufchatel cheese shaped into pearls and rolled in toasted coconut or toasted, finely chopped almonds.

CHEESY TATO SALAD

To perk up ordinary potato salad, add chopped hard-cooked eggs, sliced pitted olives, and sweet pickle relish and toss thoroughly. Sprinkle bits of crumbled Gorgonzola or Bleu cheese on top and surround with sliced of Gouda, Bonbel, and sharp Cheddar for a pretty platter. Decorate with parsley springs.

GRILLED MUENSTER CHEESEWICH

Spread two slices of white bread with mustard. Place on one a slice of Muenster and sprinkle it with ½ teaspoon of poppy seeds. Cover that with another slice of Muenster and close the sandwich. Cream 1 teaspoon of onion flakes or chopped fresh onions with 2 teaspoons of butter for each sandwich. Spread the "cheesewich" top with the butter mixture and grill. So good they'll ask for it again and again!

OPEN FACE HAVARTI CHEESEWICH

Top a toasted slice of whole wheat bread with a generous slice of Havarti or Muenster. Return to oven or microwave to melt cheese. Top with a slice of crisp fried bacon.

Havarti is a wonderful, buttery good cheese--treat yourself to its delightful taste.

TIP! The "firm" cheeses (like Cheddar, Gruyere, Edam) will keep six months, eight months, even a year or more, Process cheeses will keep indefinitely. The "semi-firm" cheeses (like Port-Salut, etc.) will keep in the refrigerator for as long as two months. The "soft-ripening" and "fresh" (or uncured) cheeses (like Brie, Camembert, Boursin) will keep as long as a month.

HOT TURKEY CHEESEWICHES

1 cup chopped cooked turkey
¼ cup chopped onion
½ cup mayonnaise or
  salad dressing
2 teaspoons prepared mustard
6 slices bread, toasted
6 slices Swiss cheese

Combine turkey, onion, mayonnaise and mustard in medium mixing bowl; mix well. Spread equal amount of turkey mixture on each toasted bread slice. Top with cheese slice. Arrange on paper towel. Microwave on Roast (Medium High) 1½-2 minutes or until cheese is melted. Teenagers love this!

CHEDDAR BUTTER SPREAD

½ cup butter, softened
1 cup (4 ounces) finely
  grated Cheddar cheese
½ teaspoon Worcestershire
¼ teaspoon garlic salt

In small bowl, combine all ingredients. Serve with warm bread. Makes 1½ cups. Makes quick hors d'oeuvres on Melba toast or crackers for drop-in guests.

DELICATE FRENCH ONION SOUP

¼ cup butter or margarine
3 cups thinly sliced onion rings
1 can beef bouillon
1 can chicken bouillon
½ cup water
½ cup white wine
1 teaspoon Worcestershire sauce
½ teaspoon thyme
1 teaspoon Tony's Creole Seasoning
¼ cup shredded Parmesan
¼ cup shredded Swiss
Seasoned croutons

In 3-quart casserole, combine butter and onion rings. Microwave on High for 7 to 8 minutes or until onions are transparent. Add beef and chicken bouillon, water, wine, Worcestershire, thyme, and seasoning. Cover with lid or plastic wrap. Microwave on High 5 minutes, then on 50% power for 10-12 minutes or until onions are tender and soup is hot. Serve in bowls topped with Parmesan and Swiss cheeses and seasoned croutons. Serves 4-6.

TIP! Cut your cheeses according to their basic shapes. Round, flat cheeses (like Brie or Port-Salut) are cut in wedges. Long "sausage-shaped" cheeses are sliced like sausages. Blocks of cheese (like Cheddar) may be cubed or sliced. Balls (like Edam or Gouda) should be cut in half, then cut from round side to flat side.

POPCORN SOUP

2 (10¾-ounce) cans Cheddar cheese soup
1 teaspoon sugar
½ teaspoon garlic salt
1/8 teaspoon pepper
¾ cup milk
½ cup beer, room temperature (strong or light)
4-6 cups popped popcorn

In medium saucepan over low heat, combine soup, sugar, garlic salt, pepper and milk. Heat to simmering. Stir in beer. Ladle into mugs or bowls. Top with generous amounts of popcorn just before serving. Serves 4-6.

HOT ARTICHOKE DIP

1 (8-ounce) package cream cheese
1 (6-ounce) jar marinated artichoke hearts
1/3 cup sour cream
2 tablespoons chopped green onion
1 tablespoon chopped pimento
1/8 teaspoon red pepper sauce

Soften cream cheese in medium glass bowl on Medium about 2 minutes. Drain artichoke hearts. Chop and add to cream cheese along with 1 tablespoon of drained liquor. Mix in remaining ingredients. Microwave at Medium 3-6 minutes or until hot, stirring several times. Serve with chips or crackers. Makes 2 cups.

HOT CHIPPED BEEF DIP

½ cup coarsely chopped pecans
2 tablespoons butter
½ teaspoon salt
11 ounces cream cheese
2 tablespoons milk
1 (2½-ounce) jar dried beef, cut in pieces
¼ cup chopped green pepper
1 small onion, grated
Pepper to taste
1 cup sour cream

Microwave pecans with butter and salt on Roast (Medium High) 3 minutes; stir; then another 2-4 minutes stirring once or twice.

Soften cream cheese and mix with milk, beef, green pepper, onion, and pepper. Fold in sour cream and half the nuts. Microwave on Medium using Probe to 115 degrees (about 2 minutes.).

TIP! Serve cheeses at room temperature. This softens the texture, releases the aroma, maximizes the flavor. Allow about an hour out of the refrigerator for most cheeses—more for Brie, Camembert, etc., which should be eaten almost "runny."

PEPPERONI 'N CHEESE CRESCENTS

1 (8-ounce) can refrigerated dinner rolls
24 slices pepperoni
4 slices Cheddar or Swiss cheese cut in half to form triangles
1 egg white

Preheat oven to 375 degrees. On ungreased cookie sheet, separate rolls into triangles. Place 3 slices of pepperoni and one slice of cheese on each roll. Start at shortest side of triangle and roll to opposite point; curve into crescent shape. Brush rolls with egg white. Bake 10-14 minutes. Makes 8 rolls.

STUFFED MUSHROOMS

½ pound large fresh mushrooms
¼ cup chopped onions
2 tablespoons butter
¼ cup seasoned bread crumbs
2 tablespoons grated Parmesan
¼ cup (2 ounces) shredded Swiss, Cheddar or Mozzarella
1 teaspoon parsley flakes
Dash salt
1/8 teaspoon pepper
¼ teaspoon dry mustard

Wash mushrooms; remove and chop stems. In a 1-quart casserole, combine chopped stem, onion and butter; cover. Microwave at High 2 minutes or until tender. Stir in remaining ingredients. Mound in mushroom caps. Arrange caps on paper towel on plate with large caps to outside. Microwave at High 2-2½ minutes or until heated through, rotating plate once or twice during cooking.

MICROWAVE CHEESE SAUCE

¼ cup butter or oleo
¼ cup flour
2 cups milk
½ teaspoon salt
1/8 teaspoon dry mustard
1/8 teaspoon pepper
Dash of paprika
2 tablespoons sherry
1 cup (4 ounces) shredded Cheddar cheese

Micromelt butter in 4-cup glass measure at High 30 seconds. Blend in flour. Stir in milk. Microwave at High 3 minutes, stirring once or twice, or until thick and smooth. Stir in seasonings, sherry, and grated cheese. Microwave at High another 45 seconds. Stir well to blend cheese into sauce.

Use as a sauce over vegetables, a topping for crepes, or stir into hot cooked macaroni or noodles.

TIP! When making a cheese sauce, add the cheese to the other ingredients at the last minute. Allow the sauce to cook only until the cheese melts. When reheating cheese sauces, warm them over hot water.

BLEU CHEESE SAUCE

¼ cup butter or margarine
4 tablespoons flour
1 clove garlic, minced
1 cup Half-and-Half cream
1½ cups chicken broth
4 ounces Bleu cheese, crumbled

Heat butter in pan. Stir in flour and garlic and cook until bubbly. Gradually stir in Half-and-Half and chicken broth, stirring until thickened. Add Bleu cheese and stir till blended. Delicious on meats and vegetables.

ASPARAGUS ROLL-UPS

18 slices of thin-sliced bread
1 (8-ounce) package Roquefort, softened
1 (8-ounce) package cream cheese, softened
1 egg
1 tablespoon mayonnaise
1 can asparagus spears
½ cup butter, melted

Cut crust from bread and roll flat. Make smooth mixture of cheeses, egg and mayonnaise. Spread on bread. Roll 1 stalk of asparagus in each slice of bread and cut into 3 pieces. Dip each piece into melted butter. Seams may need to be secured with a toothpick. Bake at 350 degrees 15 minutes or until browned. Makes 72 pieces. Delicious for morning bridge.

TIP! After cutting a crumbly-type cheese, draw the flat of the knife across the cut surface to close its "pores" and prevent moisture loss.

EASY SOUFFLE

1 cup shredded sharp Cheddar cheese
6 eggs, separated
1 (10¾-ounce) can cream of celery soup

Preheat oven to 300 degrees. Combine soup and cheese in a large saucepan. Heat slowly, stirring occasionally, until cheese is melted; remove from heat. Beat egg whites in a large bowl until soft peaks form. Beat egg yolks in a medium-size bowl until thick and lemon colored; gradually stir in soup mixture. Fold egg yolk-soup mixture gently into whites until no streaks of white remain. Pour mixture into ungreased 2-quart casserole. Bake for 1 hour or until souffle is puffed and golden and fairly firm to the touch. Serve immediately. Makes 4-6 servings. Easy and good!

CHEESY POTATO CASSEROLE

1 pound frozen hash brown potatoes, thawed
½ teaspoon salt
¼ teaspoon pepper
¼ cup chopped onion
½ (10¾-ounce) can cream of chicken soup
1½ cups grated sharp Cheddar cheese
1 cup sour cream

Reserve ½ cup grated cheese. Mix remainder of ingredients and put in greased casserole. Sprinkle reserved cheese on top. Bake uncovered at 350 degrees 45 minutes. Serves 6.

SPINACH LARRAINE

2 (10-ounce) packages frozen chopped spinach
4 tablespoons butter
2 tablespoons chopped onion
2 tablespoons flour
½ cup evaporated milk or light cream
½ cup vegetable liquor
¾ teaspoon celery salt
¾ teaspoon garlic salt
1 teaspoon Worcestershire
Salt and pepper to taste
1 (6-ounce) roll garlic cheese, Jalapena or Monterey Jack

Cook spinach according to microwave directions. Drain and save liquor. Micromelt butter on High 50 seconds. Saute chopped onions about 2 minutes or until soft. Add flour, evaporated milk and vegetable liquor. Microwave on High 2½-3½ minutes or until thickened, stirring after 2 minutes and then every minute. Add seasonings. Stir in cut-up cheese until melted. Mix with spinach and turn into buttered casserole; top with dry bread crumbs if desired. Microwave on High about 6-7 minutes or until bubbly and heated through.

BROILED PARMESAN TOMATOES

Slice top off whole tomatoes. Sprinkle with freshly grated Parmesan cheese, parsley and seasoned bread crumbs. Broil until cheese is browned.

TIP! For easy cleanup, oil the grater before grating cheese. Roquefort will grate easier if put in freezer 30 minutes before grating.

ZUCCHINI ZELICIOUS

2 tablespoons butter
2 teaspoons parsley
2 tablespoons chopped onion
½ pound fresh mushrooms, sliced
2 medium zucchini, thinly sliced
1 large ripe tomato, diced
1 teaspoon salt
¼ teaspoon cayenne pepper
¼ teaspoon garlic powder
1 cup (8 ounces) grated Cheddar cheese
½ cup seasoned bread crumbs

In a 3-quart casserole, micromelt butter. Add parsley and onion. Saute on High 2 minutes. Add mushrooms and saute on High 2 more minutes. Add zucchini, tomato, and seasonings. Cover with waxed paper. Cook on High 5 minutes. Stir in cheese. Top with bread crumbs. Cover with waxed paper. Cook on High another 5 minutes or until desired tenderness. Serves 6.

HARRY'S FAVORITE CASSEROLE

1 cup soda cracker crumbs
2 cups medium white sauce
½ pound American cheese, grated
1 (7-ounce) can pimento, chopped
4 hard-boiled eggs, grated
Buttered cracker crumbs

In greased 8x8x2-inch baking dish, place a layer of crumbs and moisten with half of white sauce. Layer cheese, pimento and grated eggs; repeat layers; top with buttered crumbs. Bake at 350 degrees about 25 minutes. Harry even loves this for breakfast! (And it was a favorite of President Eisenhower!).

SAVORY MASHED POTATO CASSEROLE

1½ cups water
½ teaspoon salt
2 tablespoons butter or oleo
½ cup milk
1½ cups potato flakes
½ cup sour cream
½ teaspoon onion salt
1 egg
1 cup shredded sharp Cheddar cheese

Combine water, salt and butter in 1½-quart glass casserole. Cover with glass lid or plastic wrap. Microwave on High 3-4 minutes or until mixture bubbles. Stir in milk and potato flakes. Blend in sour cream, onion salt, and egg. Mix well. Sprinkle with cheese. Recover. Microwave on Roast (Medium High) 6-8 minutes or until hot. Let stand, covered, 3 minutes before serving. Serves 4-6.

Note: 3 cups fresh, mashed potatoes may be substituted for potato flakes. Add only sour cream, onion salt, egg and cheese.

To make ahead, prepare as directed through *Recover.* Cover with plastic wrap and refrigerate. At serving time, Microwave on Roast 10-12 minutes.

OLE! RICE CASSEROLE

1 cup long grain rice
10 ounces sharp Cheddar cheese
1 cup sour cream
1 (3-ounce) can chopped green chilies (not hot)

Cook rice according to directions. Let cool. Grate cheese and reserve 1/3 for top of casserole. Mix rice, sour cream and green chilies. Pour ½ of mixture into greased casserole and top with cheese, then add rest of mixture. Top with reserved cheese. Cook at 300 degrees for 30 minutes or until bubbly. Ole!

ITALIAN PARCHEESI PASTA

1 pound ground beef
1 (32-ounce) jar spaghetti sauce
1 cup water
1½ teaspoons salt
1 (15-ounce) container Ricotta cheese

2 tablespoons grated Parmesan
2 eggs
¼ teaspoon pepper
1 (8-ounce) package shredded Mozzarella (2 cups)
1 (8-ounce) package manicotti, uncooked

About 1 hour before serving, crumble ground beef in a 2-quart casserole. Cook on High, uncovered, for 5-6 minutes or until meat is no longer pink, stirring after half the cooking time. Drain. Stir in spaghetti sauce, water and 1 teaspoon salt. Cover with plastic wrap. Cook on High for 4-6 minutes, again stirring after half the cooking time.

In a medium bowl, combine Ricotta and Parmesan cheeses, eggs, pepper, 1½ cups Mozzarella cheese, and ½ teaspoon salt. Mix well. Stuff manicotti with cheese filling. In a 9x13-inch baking dish, arrange manicotti in single layer; add meat sauce to completely cover. Sprinkle with remaining Mozzarella. Cover dish with plastic wrap. Cook on Medium-high for 30-35 minutes, rotating dish half-turn during cooking. Let stand 5 minutes. Makes 7 servings.

CHICKEN ALA ROMANO

1 whole chicken breast, split, boned and skinned
1 slice Swiss cheese, halved
1 thin slice prosciutto or smoked ham, halved
3 tablespoons dry breadcrumbs

1 tablespoon grated Romano
1 teaspoon paprika
1/8 teaspoon garlic salt
Pinch of dried whole tarragon
2 tablespoons butter or oleo

Place chicken breast half on a sheet of waxed paper; flatten to ¼-inch thickness, using a meat mallet or rolling pin. Place a piece of Swiss cheese and prosciutto in center of each piece of chicken. Roll up lengthwise and secure with a wooden pick.

Combine next 5 ingredients, stirring well. Place butter in 1-cup glass measure; microwave on High 40 seconds to melt. Dip each chicken breast half in butter; roll in crumb mixture.

Place rolls, seam side down, ia a 1-quart shallow casserole. Cover with waxed paper and microwave on High 4 minutes or until chicken is fork tender, rotating dish after 2 minutes. Serves 2. A must to try. Superb!

QUICK-FIX PARMESAN FISH

1 pound mild white fish
¼ teaspoon seasoned salt
2 tablespoons butter or oleo
½ cup grated Parmesan

½ cup mayonnaise
2 tablespoons chopped green
 onions
Paprika

Wipe and dry fish. Arrange fish in a 12x8-inch glass baking dish. Sprinkle with seasoned salt. Dot with butter. Cover with waxed paper. Microwave on High 2 minutes.

Blend Parmesan cheese, mayonnaise, onions. Spread cheese mixture over fish. Cover with waxed paper. Microwave on High 2-3 minutes. Sprinkle with paprika before serving. Serves 3-4.

MAMA MIA MEATLOAF

1½ pounds lean ground beef
½ cup dry bread crumbs
1 (8 ounce) can tomato
 sauce, divided
1 egg
1 teaspoon oregano, divided

1 teaspoon salt
1/8 teaspoon pepper
1½ cups shredded Mozzarella
 or Monterey Jack
2 tablespoons grated Parmesan

Mix together ground beef, bread crumbs, half the tomato sauce, egg, ½ teaspoon oregano, salt and pepper. On waxed paper, shape into a rectangle ½-inch thick. Sprinkle with cheese, leaving ½-inch border. Roll up starting on short side. Roll with paper till tight, then peel paper back. Seal edges and place in loaf dish. Microwave on High 9 minutes. Reduce power to medium and turn dish. Microwave 11-14 minutes or until meat loses its pink color. Drain.

Combine remaining tomato sauce and oregano. Pour over meat loaf. Sprinkle with Parmesan cheese. Microwave at Medium High about 2 minutes to heat sauce. Cover with foil and let stand 5 minutes before serving. Serves 4-6.

BRANDY ALEXANDER SOUFFLE

2 ounces unflavored gelatin
½ cup cold water
1½ cups hot water
4 eggs, separated
¾ cup sugar
1 (8-ounce) package cream cheese, softened

3 tablespoons creme de cacao
3 tablespoons brandy
¼ cup sugar
1 cup heavy cream, whipped
Chocolate curls (optional)
Chocolate shavings (optional)

Cut a piece of aluminum foil to fit around a 1½-quart souffle dish, allowing a 1-inch overlap; fold lengthwise into thirds. Lightly oil one side of the foil; wrap around outside of dish, oiled side against dish, allowing it to extend 3 inches above rim to form a collar. Secure with freezer tape.

Soften gelatin in cold water; stir. In a separate 2½-quart casserole, microwave 1½ cups hot water at High for 5-9 minutes till boiling. Add gelatin mixture, stirring to dissolve. Beat egg yolks until thick and lemon colored; gradually add ¾ cup sugar, beating well. Gradually stir in about ¼ of the hot gelatin mixture; then stir into remaining hot mixture. Microwave at High 2-3 minutes or until thickened, stirring after 2 minutes.

Beat cream cheese until smooth; gradually add yolk mixture, beating well. Stir in creme de cacao and brandy; chill until slightly thickened.

Beat egg whites until foamy; gradually add ¼ cup sugar, beating until stiff peaks form. Gently fold whipped cream and beaten egg whites into cream cheese mixture. Spoon mixture into collared souffle dish; chill until formed. Serve in champagne glasses. Garnish with chocolate curls and shavings. Serves 8-10.

MINT CHOCOLATE PARFAIT PIE

1 (8-ounce package) cream cheese, softened
¾ cup sugar
2 eggs
2 ounces unsweetened chocolate, melted

¼ teaspoon peppermint extract
1 cup whipping cream, whipped or 2 cups prepared whipped topping
1 (9-inch) pie shell, baked

In a large bowl, beat cream cheese and sugar until fluffy. Add eggs one at a time beating well after each addition. Blend in chocolate and extract. Carefully fold in whipped cream. Spoon into baked, cooled pie shell. Chill several hours. Serve with additional whipped cream, if desired. Refrigerate leftovers. Serves 8.

The Country Mouse in her Country House

*The Country Mouse is quite innovative and wise
In planning a meatless meal that satisfies.*

*Cheese sauces enhance spinach, beans and potatoes
And go quite well with farm fresh tomatoes.*

*Casseroles of eggs, cheese, and no meat
Cost less and are a real taste treat!*

DELICIOUS BRUNCH PIE

1 (10-ounce) package frozen chopped broccoli, chopped spinach or asparagus spears, cooked and drained
1 cup sour cream
1 cup creamed cottage cheese
½ cup Bisquick baking mix
¼ cup margarine or butter, melted
2 eggs
1 tomato, peeled and thinly sliced
¼ cup grated Parmesan cheese

Heat oven to 350 degrees. Grease pie plate; spread broccoli in plate. Beat sour cream, cottage cheese, baking mix, margarine and eggs until smooth, 15 seconds in blender on high or 1 minute with hand beater. Pour into plate. Top with tomatoes; sprinkle with Parmesan cheese. Bake until knife inserted between center and edge comes out clean, about 30 minutes. Cool 5 minutes. Serves 6 to 8. Yummy!

NANCY'S CHEESY WAFFLES

1¼ cups self-rising flour
1 tablespoon sugar
1 1/8 cups milk
3/8 cup vegetable oil
1 egg separated
½ cup grated Cheddar cheese
Bacon bits

In bowl combine flour and sugar. Add milk, oil and yolk mixture to flour; stir to blend. Fold in stiffly beaten egg white.
    Pour a dipper of batter on hot waffle iron. Sprinkle a tablespoon or so of grated cheese and ½ teaspoon of bacon bits on top and cook until light brown. Makes 5-6 waffles. With or without butter and syrup, these are light, fluffy and delicious!

FARMER'S GARDEN SALAD

Arrange Farmer or Havarti cheese on a bed of crisp greens. For a particularly attractive salad luncheon, surround it with either tiny whole pickled beets, ripe olives, tiny carrot sticks, small sweet gherkins, bright red apple slices, pitted prunes, or mandarin orange sections—or any combination. Serve with French dressing.

COUNTRY SLAW

1 medium head cabbage, shredded
1 (8-ounce) can crushed pineapple, drained
1 cup (4 ounces) shredded sharp Cheddar cheese
¾ cup raisins
1 cup mayonnaise

Combine all in a large mixing bowl; stir gently. Chill 1-2 hours before serving. Serves 8-10. Better the second day—if there is any left! Really good!

RINKTUM DIDDY

1 tablespoon butter or oleo
1 medium onion, chopped
1 (10¼-ounce) can tomato soup
1 cup (8 ounces) cheese, cut in small cubes
2 eggs
Salt and red pepper

Saute onion in butter. Place in double boiler and add soup. Stir in cheese till melted. Season and stir in lightly beaten eggs. Cook until thick. Serve hot over crackers. Nice supper dish!

DOWN HOME CHEDDAR CHEESE SOUP

½ cup margarine
½ cup each finely chopped: celery, green pepper, onion, carrot, cauliflower
1 tablespoon granulated chicken bouillon or 2 cubes
2 cups water
½ cup margarine
2/3 cup flour
4 cups milk
½ pound sharp Cheddar cheese, shredded

Heat margarine over medium heat. Add vegetables; cook until tender, stirring often. Add water and chicken bouillon; heat to boiling. Cover; cook over low heat 10 minutes. Meanwhile, heat remaining margarine in saucepan. Stir in flour; cook until bubbly. Remove from heat. Gradually stir in milk. Cook over medium heat, stirring often, until thickened, but do not boil. Stir in cheese till fully blended. Stir cheese mixture into vegetables and chicken broth mixture. Serves 8-10. Flavor is outstanding.

SWISS LIMA CASSEROLE

4 cups fresh lima beans
¼ cup butter or margarine
3 tablespoons flour
2½ cups milk
2 cups (8 ounces) shredded Swiss cheese
1 (4-ounce) can sliced mushrooms, drained
3 tablespoons grated onion
½ cup sliced almonds, lightly toasted

Cook beans in boiling, salted water till tender (20-30 minutes); drain. Melt butter in heavy saucepan over low heat; add flour and cook 1 minute, stirring constantly. Gradually add milk. Cook over medium heat, stirring constantly, until thickened and bubbly. Add cheese; stir until cheese melts. Combine beans, mushrooms, and onion in a deep 2-quart casserole; stir gently. Pour cheese sauce over bean mixture; sprinkle with almonds. Bake at 350 degrees 20-30 minutes or until bubbly. Serves 8.

BARN DANCE DISH

1 pound fresh mushrooms
¼ pound Cheddar cheese (plus a little)
1 (8-ounce) can pitted black olives
1½ tablespoons flour
¼ teaspoon MSG
½ teaspoon salt
1/8 teaspoon pepper
1/3 cup Half-and-Half
1½ tablespoons butter
1 cup fresh bread crumbs

Clean mushrooms and slice lengthwise through the stems. Shred cheese. Drain canned olives and slice or coarsely chop. In a greased 2-quart casserole, arrange mushrooms, cheese, and olives in alternate layers. Blend together flour, MSG, salt and pepper, and add Half-and-Half, and pour over mushrooms. In a small pan, melt butter; add bread crumbs and spread over top of casserole. Bake at 350 degrees until bubbly and golden brown, about 30 minutes. Serves 6.

FLUFFY POTATO CASSEROLE

4 large Idaho potatoes, baked
¾ cup butter
1 tablespoon salt
1 cup whipping cream
1 teaspoon black pepper
Chopped chives, optional
Grated Gruyere or Cheddar cheese (1 cup or more)

Scoop hot potatoes from their shells and mix with all other ingredients except the cheese. Place in 2-quart casserole, dot with additional butter, and sprinkle with cheese. Bake at 375 degrees 15-20 minutes. Serves 6-8.

CHEESEASY CAULIFLOWER

1 large cauliflower
1½ cups cream
Salt and pepper to taste

1 cup (4 ounces) grated Gruyere or sharp Cheddar or Longhorn

Cut cauliflower into flowerets and cook in boiling, salted water 5 minutes. Drain. Place in an ovenproof dish. Season cream with salt and pepper and pour over cauliflower. Cover with cheese and bake in 450-degree oven 20 minutes. Serves 6-8.

SPINACH WITH CREAM CHEESE

2 pounds fresh spinach
¼ cup water
½ teaspoon salt
2 tablespoons butter
1 (8-ounce) bar cream cheese

2 tablespoons chopped chives
1/8 teaspoon garlic powder
2 hard-boiled eggs, grated
Paprika

Wash spinach thoroughly, making sure all sand is washed from leaves. In a large saucepan, bring water to a boil and add the salt and spinach. Cover and cook over low heat until leaves are limp. Do not overcook.

Cut cream cheese into small cubes and add to the spinach, along with chives and garlic powder. Cook until cheese melts, stirring occasionally. Place spinach in a heated serving bowl and top with grated eggs. Sprinkle with paprika and serve immediately. This is a pretty and easily-prepared side dish. Serves 4-6.

PARMESAN CHEESE SOUFFLE

½ cup flour
1 cup light cream
2 tablespoons butter
1 cup (4 ounces) grated Parmesan cheese

4 egg yolks
½ teaspoon salt
1/8 teaspoon white pepper
4 egg whites

In a saucepan, mix flour with cream until very smooth. Add butter and cook over low heat stirring constantly until mixture reaches boiling point. Cook 5 minutes longer, stirring occasionally. Mix in cheese till melted. Cool, then beat in 1 egg yolk at a time. Stir in salt and pepper. Beat egg whites till stiff but not dry, and fold into cheese mixture.

Turn into a 1½-quart buttered, souffle dish. Place dish in a pan containing 2 inches of water and bake in a preheated 375-degree oven 45 minutes. Serve immediately. Serves 4.

COUNTRY CORN PUDDING

2 tablespoons butter
2 tablespoons salad oil
½ onion, finely chopped
1 cup whole kernel corn, canned (drained) or fresh
1 tablespoon sugar
Salt and pepper to taste
½ cup (4 ounces) shredded Cheddar cheese
3 eggs, separated

Heat butter and salad oil in skillet. Saute onion; add corn, sugar, salt and pepper. Cool and add cheese and well-beaten egg yolks. Fold in stiffly beaten egg whites. Pour in well-greased 9x11 casserole and set in pan of hot water. Bake in 350-degree oven 1 hour. Serve at once. Serves 4-6.

MUENSTROUSLY DELICIOUS ONION CASSEROLE

2 tablespoons butter
2 large sweet Spanish onions, sliced, separated into rings
2 cups (8 ounces) grated Muenster cheese
¼ teaspoon pepper
1 (10¾-ounce) can cream of chicken soup
Sliced, buttered, slightly dry French bread

Melt butter in large frying pan. Add onion rings. Cover and cook slowly over low heat, stirring often, for 20-30 minutes or until soft. Spoon into a 6-cup, fairly shallow baking dish. Spread cheese over top and sprinkle with pepper. Heat soup and milk in same frying pan in which onions were cooked, stirring until smooth. Pour over onion-cheese layer. Stir lightly with tip of knife to let sauce flow to bottom. Overlap enough bread slices, buttered side up, to make a ring around top. Bake in 350-degree oven 30 minutes or until bread is toasted and sauce is hot. Serves 6-8.

OLD-FASHIONED MACARONI AND CHEESE BAKE

1 cup raw macaroni
2 cups (8 ounces) grated sharp Cheddar cheese
2 eggs
2/3 cup milk
½ teaspoon salt
¼ teaspoon paprika
Cayenne to taste
¼ cup dry bread crumbs
3 tablespoons butter

Parboil macaroni in salted water; drain. In buttered casserole, layer macaroni and 1½ cups cheese. Beat eggs, milk and seasonings well. Pour over layered macaroni and cheese. Sprinkle with crumbs, dot with butter and top with remaining ½ cup cheese. Bake at 350 degrees 20 minutes or until knife inserted in middle comes clean. Serves 4.

BAKED POTATO BOATS

6 medium baking potatoes
2/3 cup milk
1 egg

2 cups sharp Cheddar, grated
4 tablespoons butter or oleo
Salt, cayenne pepper to taste

Scrub potatoes, then bake in 350-degree oven 1½ hours. Cut in half lengthwise; gently spoon out flesh, reserving skin "boats." Bring milk to boil then beat into potatoes until smooth. Beat in egg, cheese, butter, salt and cayenne. Spoon mixture into potato skins, sprinkle with more cheese and bake in a 350-degree oven 15 minutes. Before serving, add a tall, thin triangle of cheese to form sail. Six mates can probably eat two apiece!

EGGPLANT PROVOLONE

1 large eggplant
1 medium onion, chopped
2 cups (or 1 can) tomatoes, chopped
½ teaspoon salt
Dash pepper

2 cups leftover cornbread or crackers, crumbled
2 eggs, slightly beaten
2 tablespoons milk
2 cups (8 ounces) shredded Provolone

Cut up peeled eggplant and steam with onion in a little water on low heat till tender; drain. Mix remaining ingredients with eggplant, saving a few tablespoons of Provolone for the top. More milk may be needed to give mixture thick batter consistency. Place in buttered casserole and sprinkle remaining Provolone on top. Place in 375-degree oven until brown and bubbly. Cheddar may be substituted, but the Provolone is really special!

ZUCCHINI-TOMATO PIE

2 cups chopped zucchini
1 cup chopped tomatoes
½ cup chopped onion
1/3 cup (3 ounces) grated Parmesan cheese

1½ cups milk
¾ cup Bisquick baking mix
3 eggs
½ teaspoon salt
¼ teaspoon pepper

Heat oven to 400 degrees. Grease 10-inch quiche dish or pie plate. Sprinkle zucchini, tomato, onion, and cheese in plate. Beat remaining ingredients until smooth, 15 seconds in blender or 1 minute with hand beater. Pour into plate. Bake until knife inserted in center comes out clean, about 30 minutes. Cool 5 minutes. Serves 6.

SUPPERTIME CELERY

3 cups diced green celery
½ cup toasted, slivered almonds
½ teaspoon salt
1/8 teaspoon white pepper
½ stick butter or oleo, melted
2 cups (8 ounces) grated sharp Cheddar cheese
2 cups basic white sauce
½ cup (2 ounces) grated sharp Cheddar cheese for topping

Into a 2-quart casserole, place ingredients in order listed. Bake about 50-60 minutes at 250 degrees. Serves 6. Simply delicious, whether you are a celery lover or not!

BASIC WHITE SAUCE:

½ stick butter or oleo
¼ cup flour
½ teaspoon salt
2 cups milk

Melt butter in saucepan. Stir in flour and salt. Stir in milk gradually. Continue to stir over medium heat until smooth and slightly thickened. Serve warm over casserole.

MEATLESS COTTAGE CHEESE MEATLOAF

2 cups creamed cottage cheese
3 eggs, beaten
¼ cup milk
½ cup chopped onion
2 bouillon cubes, shaved, or equivalent amount
¼ cup cooking oil
½ cup finely chopped pecans
4½ cups cereal flakes
½ cup shredded sharp Cheddar cheese
2 tablespoons sour cream

Beat together cottage cheese, eggs and milk. Add remaining ingredients; mix very well. Place in an oiled loaf pan. Bake at 375 degrees 45 minutes. Serve hot or cold. Makes 12 servings. This has the texture and flavor of meatloaf.

COUNTRY CHEESE CORN BREAD

1½ cups self-rising corn meal
1 cup cream corn
1½ cups grated mild Cheddar cheese
1 medium onion, chopped
1 cup milk
2 eggs
½ cup oil
1 teaspoon sugar

Mix all ingredients together. Pour into a greased and heated 12-inch skillet. Bake at 350 degrees 30-40 minutes or until golden brown.

SILO BREAD

1 package active dry yeast
¼ cup hot tap water
2 1/3 cups flour
2 tablespoons sugar
1 teaspoon salt

¼ teaspoon soda
1 cup sour cream
1 egg
1 cup shredded Cheddar cheese
½ teaspoon pepper

Grease two 1-pound coffee cans. In large mixer bowl, dissolve yeast in hot water. Add 1 1/3 cups flour, sugar, salt, soda, sour cream and egg. Blend ½ minute on low speed, scraping bowl constantly. Beat 2 minutes at high speed, scraping bowl occasionally. Stir in remaining flour, cheese and pepper thoroughly.

Divide batter between cans. Let rise in warm place 50 minutes. (Batter will rise slightly but will not double.) Heat oven to 350 degrees. Bake 40 minutes or until golden brown. Immediately remove from cans. Cool slightly before slicing.

CHEESE POPOVER PUFFS

1 cup flour
½ teaspoon salt
1 cup milk
2 eggs

1 tablespoon butter or oleo, melted
¼ cup (2 ounces) shredded Cheddar cheese

Heat oven to 425 degrees. Generously grease 6-8 muffin cups or popover pan. In small mixing bowl, combine flour, salt, milk, butter and eggs. Beat with rotary beater or slowest speed of mixer until smooth. Stir in cheese. Fill prepared cups 2/3 full. Bake 15 minutes at 425 degrees, then reduce oven temperature to 350 degrees. Bake 35 minutes longer until golden brown. Prick with a sharp knife during last 5 minutes to allow escape of steam. Serve immediately. Judy fills these with sour cream after baking and they are delicious!

FROZEN PEANUT BUTTER PIE

4 ounces cream cheese
½ cup powdered sugar
1/3 cup crunchy peanut butter
½ cup milk
8 ounces whipped topping
¼ cup salted peanuts, finely chopped
1 (9-inch) graham cracker crust or regular crust

Whip softened cream cheese till creamy. Beat in powdered sugar and peanut butter. Slowly add milk, blending thoroughly. Fold in topping and pour into pie shell. Sprinkle with chopped peanuts and freeze until firm. Take directly from freezer to cut and serve. Makes a large pie. Double the recipe to make 3 medium-sized pies. Delicious! Children particularly like this.

CHEDDAR CHEESE PIE

3 eggs
1½ cups (6 ounces) grated Cheddar cheese
1½ cups sugar
½ teaspoon salt
1 teaspoon flour
1 teaspoon vanilla
1 teaspoon grated orange rind
1 cup milk
1 (9-inch) pastry shell, unbaked

Separate eggs and whip whites until stiff. Mix all other ingredients well. Fold in stiffly beaten egg whites. Pour into an unbaked pastry shell and bake in a 300-degree oven 35 minutes or until top browns and pie is set. Sharp Cheddar makes it even better! The flavor is unique and a very pleasant surprise!

TIP! To heat frozen cheese dishes, cover them tightly with foil and place in a moderate oven.

CAROL'S CHERRY CHEESECAKE

1 pound cream cheese, softened
¾ cup sugar
1 teaspoon vanilla
3 eggs, separated
1 (21-ounce) can cherry pie filling
1 graham cracker crust

Mix by hand cream cheese, sugar, vanilla, and egg yolks until light. Beat egg whites until stiff; fold into cream mixture. Pour cherry pie filling into crust; cover with cheese mixture. Bake at 350 degrees 40-60 minutes until nicely browned. Delicious!

The Country Mouse Has a Wine and Cheese Party

*Hurray! Yippee! It's time again
To have all the friends and neighbors in.*

*The Country Mouse has a special menu that pleases
Wine and a great big assortment of cheeses!*

*She'll need a variety of red, rosé and white
She checks the wine chart to order just right!*

CAROL'S SPECIAL STUFFED CELERY

6-8 celery stalks
1 (8-ounce) package cream cheese, softened
2 ounces Bleu cheese
Salt to taste
Pepper, Cayenne pepper
Dash of sugar
Juice of ½ small onion
1 teaspoon Worcestershire
½ teaspoon lemon juice
2-3 drops Tabasco
1 tablespoon mayonnaise
1 tablespoon Half-and-Half

Clean and strip celery and cut into 5-inch lengths. Drain on paper towels. Mix cheeses till smooth. Add seasonings and onion juice and cream well. Add Worcestershire, lemon juice and Tabasco. Mix mayonnaise and cream together until smooth but not runny; add to cheese mixture. Spread mixture in celery and sprinkle with paprika. Refrigerate till hard; serve on salad tray.

CHEESE AND FRUIT CENTERPIECE

1 honeydew or canteloupe melon
Red apples
Lemon juice
Seedless green grapes
Whole strawberries
Green pears
Cheeses: Bleu or Roquefort; Brie or Camembert; Swiss or Jarlsberg; Gouda or Edam

Cut and peel wedges of melon and arrange in a circle in center of a large board. Put slices of unpeeled apples (sprinkled with lemon juice to prevent discoloring) and small bunches of seedless grapes between wedges of melon. Put whole strawberries in the hollow of each wedge of melon. Arrange additional bunches of grapes, strawberries and wedges of unpeeled pear in center of board. Surround fruit with wedges of assorted cheeses.

SMOKEHOUSE SHRIMP BALL

1 (8-ounce) bar cream cheese
2 (4¼-ounce) cans shrimp, washed and drained
1 tablespoon lemon juice
2 tablespoons grated onion
1 tablespoon prepared horseradish
¼ teaspoon liquid smoke
¼ teaspoon salt
½ cup chopped pecans

Cream cheese and combine with all other ingredients except pecans. Chill until firm and then shape into a ball and roll in chopped pecans.

NUTTY BLEU CHICKEN LOG

2 (8-ounce) packages cream cheese, softened
4 ounces Bleu cheese
1/3 cup finely chopped celery
1½ cups minced cooked chicken
¼ cup finely chopped toasted pecans

Beat cream cheese and Bleu cheese until smooth. Stir in celery and chicken. Shape into a log. Chill 4 hours or overnight. Roll in pecans. Serve with crackers.

BACON-ONION CHEESE LOG

Blend together 8 ounces cream cheese, ½ cup butter, Lawry's Bacon-Onion Dip Mix and 1 teaspoon poppy seeds; chill until fairly firm. Shape into 1 large or 2 small logs. Roll in minced parsley and poppy seeds to garnish. Refrigerate several hours. Remove 20 minutes before serving with crackers or dark bread.

MEXICALLY ROLL

Between 2 large pieces of waxed paper, roll 1 pound softened Velveeta to 1/8-inch thickness. With a spatula, spread 8 ounces soft cream cheese over top. Mix 1 envelope dry onion soup mix, ½ cup finely chopped pecans and 2-4 tablespoons Jalapeno pepper sauce (2 Jalapeno peppers sliced, seeds removed, 1 tablespoons Jalapeno juice). Spread over cream cheese. Roll up into a log. Refrigerate until firm. Serve with round crackers.

HAVARTI PARTY DIP

Combine 1 cup shredded Havarti with ½ cup soft Bleu cheese. Add 1 cup mayonnaise, ¼ teaspoon Worcestershire and 12 finely chopped salad olives and blend well. Serve with crackers.

PINEAPPLE CHEESE SCULPTURE

1½ pounds sharp Cheddar cheese, grated
½ pound Swiss cheese, grated
1 (3-ounce) package cream cheese, softened
¼ pound Bleu cheese, crumbled
½ cup soft butter or oleo
½ cup apple juice
2 tablespoons lemon juice
1 tablespoon Worcestershire
Whole cloves
Paprika
1 leafy crown from a large, fresh pineapple

The day before serving, combine cheeses with butter in large bowl of electric mixer. Slowly beat in apple and lemon juices and Worcestershire. Continue beating, scraping down sides of bowl often, about 5 minutes till well blended. Cover and chill several hours or until firm enough to handle.

Shape cheese mixture with your hands into a "standing pineapple" on a plate. Smooth top flat and cover whole with foil or waxed paper. Chill several hours or until very firm.

Day of serving, allow ample time for "sculpturing." Mark cheese with tip of teaspoon or toothpick to resemble a pineapple. This requires crisscross lines which form diamond shapes. Center each diamond with a whole clove; lightly sprinkle cheese with paprika. Lift mold onto a serving plate with a spatula. Place pineapple crown on top of mold; hold in place with toothpicks, if needed. Frame with a variety of crackers and parsley.

Slices of pimento-stuffed olives may be substituted for the cloves. Great for large cocktail parties. Serves 50. Pretty, too!

TIP! Before serving, cut and trim edges of past servings. The same knife that is used for sharp cheese should not be used for mild.

COOL SHRIMP DIP

½ pint sour cream
1 (8-ounce) package cream cheese, softened
½ cup diced celery
½ cup diced onions
Juice of 1 lemon
Salt and white pepper to taste
Red pepper to taste
2 (4¼-ounce) cans shrimp (or fresh boiled shrimp, if available)

Combine sour cream with cream cheese. Add celery, onions, lemon juice, salt, pepper, and red pepper. Mash the shrimp with a fork and add to the cheese mixture. Sprinkle red pepper on top and serve. This recipe will make approximately 1 quart.

MARVELOUS SEAFOOD MORNAY

1 stick butter
1 small bunch green onions, chopped
½ cup finely chopped parsley
2 tablespoons flour
1 pint Half and Half
½ pound grated Swiss cheese
1 tablespoon sherry
Red pepper to taste
Salt to taste
1 pound white crabmeat or boiled and deveined shrimp

Melt butter in heavy pot and saute onions and parsley. Blend in flour, cream and cheese until cheese is melted. Add other ingredients and gently fold in crabmeat or chopped boiled shrimp. Serve in pastry shells or in chafing dish with Melba rounds.

SALMON SUPREME

2 (16-ounce) cans pink salmon
1½ (8-ounce) packages cream cheese
2 tablespoons prepared horseradish
5 tablespoons lemon juice
4 tablespoons onion, diced
½ teaspoon salt
Parsley, chopped
Pecans, chopped
Chives, chopped
Hard-boiled egg slices

Drain salmon and mix with next five ingredients. Shape into ball. Roll in parsley, pecans and chives and place on platter. Garnish with egg slices. Serve with crackers.

A pretty garnishing idea is to mold mixture into shape of a fish. Cover head with pecans, separating head from body with thin strips of pimento. Cover body with parsley. Place egg white slices so as to resemble fins. Use sliced olive for eye and pimento for mouth.

PINEAPPLE CHEESE BALL

2 (8-ounce) packages cream cheese, softened
2 tablespoons finely chopped green pepper
2 tablespoons finely chopped onion
¼ cup drained crushed pineapple
2 teaspoons seasoned salt
2 cups chopped pecans, divided
Fresh grapes

Beat cream cheese till smooth; add green pepper, onion, pineapple, seasoned salt, and 1 cup pecans, mixing well. Shape into a ball. Roll in remaining pecans. Chill 1-2 hours. Garnish with grapes and serve with assorted crackers.

HOT CRABMEAT SPREAD

1 (8-ounce) package cream cheese
6 ounces canned, frozen or fresh crabmeat
2 tablespoons minced onion
4 tablespoons sherry or white wine
2 teaspoons horseradish
Dash of Tabasco
Dash of Worcestershire

Soften cream cheese and mix in all ingredients. Place in shallow 9x9-inch pan or 1-quart casserole. Spirinkle with paprika and bake in 350-degree oven till bubbly and light brown--about 15 minutes. Serve in chafing dish with crackers or toast.

ARTICHOKE SPREAD

1 cup mayonnaise
1 (14-ounce) can artichokes
1 cup freshly grated Parmesan cheese

Drain artichokes. Mix all ingredients with mixer in order given. Heat in moderate (350 degree) oven 20-30 minutes. Dip or spread on toast rounds.

PERFECT PIMENTO SPREAD

8 ounces sharp Cheddar cheese, grated
1 tablespoon chopped onion
1 tablespoon Worcestershire
1 (4-ounce) jar pimentos
4 tablespoons mayonnaise
Salt to taste
Red pepper to taste

Whip till fluffy. Refrigerate 24 hours. Add more mayonnaise or a little milk to soften before spreading.

HOMEMADE BOURSIN

1 (8-ounce) package cream cheese, softened
1 clove garlic, crushed
1 teaspoon basil
1 teaspoon caraway seed
1 teaspoon dill weed
1 teaspoon chives, chopped
Cracked black or lemon pepper

Blend cream cheese with garlic, caraway, basil, dill weed and chives. Pat into a round flat shape. Roll on all sides (lightly) in lemon pepper or cracked black pepper. Make a few days ahead. Serve with assorted crackers.

FRIED CHEESE

Slice very cold Mozzarella in cubes or sticks; dip in beaten egg, then in bread crumbs. Dip back in egg and breadcrumbs again being sure cheese is well covered. Fry in peanut oil in deep fryer a few at a time, turning once, till golden. Try Cheddar or a smoked cheese, frozen Camembert or leftover cheeseball. Yum!

COCKTAIL CHEESE PASTRIES

1 pound Fillo leaves *½ pound butter, melted*
½ pound Feta cheese *3 eggs*
½ pound cottage cheese *2 cups chopped parsley*

Mash cheeses; beat in 1 tablespoon melted butter, the eggs and the parsley.

Brush a pastry sheet heavily with butter. It is important to keep pastry sheets you are not working with covered with a damp towel to keep them from drying out. Cut one sheet in half crosswise, making an 8x11-inch piece. Fold into thirds lengthwise; brush top layer with butter. Place a teaspoon of the filling on one corner of the long side and fold over into a triangle, folding from one side to another until the other end is reached (as in folding a flag). Place on baking sheet and cover with plastic wrap while preparing the balance.

When all are made, brush the tops with butter, then bake in preheated 325-degree oven 30 minutes, or until golden in color. Serve warm. They may be reheated. Makes about 45.

(Fillo leaves are paper-thin 11x17-inch pieces of pastry available in most grocery stores or specialty food shops.)

SPINACH-FILLED CHEESE PASTRIES

1 medium onion, chopped *1 (10-ounce) package frozen*
¼ cup olive oil *chopped spinach*
½ teaspoons salt *1 cup feta cheese*
¼ teaspoon pepper *½ cup cottage cheese*
1 beaten egg *1 pound Fillo leaves*

Mix all ingredients (except Fillo leaves), then place ½ teaspoon on filling on one corner of the long side of the Fillo leaves; then roll up as directed in *Cocktail Cheese Pastries* recipe.

RANCH CHEESE MOUSSE

1 envelope unflavored gelatin
½ cup cold water
2 cups sour cream
1 (1½-ounce) package Hidden Valley Ranch salad dressing
½ cup crumbled Bleu cheese
1 cup small-curd cream-style cottage cheese
Parsley for garnish

Soften gelatin in cold water. Place over boiling water, stirring until gelatin dissolves. Stir dressing mix into sour cream. Add Bleu cheese and cottage cheese. Beat until well blended. Pour into 3½-cup ring mold or small loaf pan. Chill until firm.

Unmold onto platter, garnish with parsley and serve with assorted crackers. Serves 12. Gorgeous light texture!

ARTICHOKE SQUARES

2 (6-ounce) jars marinated artichokes
1 onion, chopped
1 clove garlic, minced
4 eggs
¼ cup bread crumbs
½ teaspoon oregano
2/3 cup grated Cheddar cheese
2/3 cup grated Swiss cheese
2/3 cup grated Parmesan
Dash of Tabasco
Salt and pepper to taste

Drain juice from one jar of artichokes into a skillet. Saute onion and garlic in juice. Drain second jar and chop all artichokes.

In a bowl, beat eggs; add bread crumbs, oregano, Tabasco, salt and pepper. Stir in onion, garlic, cheeses, and artichokes. Mix well. Bake in greased 9x13-inch pan 30 minutes at 325 degrees. Cut into squares. Serve hot.

TIP! When serving cheeses, cut off only as much as you intend to use. To preserve flavor and texture, let the rest stay in the refrigerator rather than warming up whole cheese and cooling it again each time.

BAKED CHICKEN NUGGETS

7-8 whole chicken breasts, boned and skinned
2 cups fine cracker crumbs
1 cup grated Parmesan
3 tablespoons Italian seasoning or 1 tablespoon each whole dried Thyme and dried basil
1 cup butter or oleo, melted

Cut chicken in 1½-inch pieces. Combine cracker crumbs and herbs; mix well. Dip chicken pieces in butter and coat with crumb mixture. Place on baking sheet in single layer. Bake at 400 degrees 20 minutes or until done. Makes 14-16 appetizers.

GOUDA WELLINGTON

½ can crescent rolls or Fillo pastry
1 (8-ounce) round Gouda, wax covering removed
Egg glaze (1 egg beaten with 2 tablespoons of water)
½ cup Jalapeno jelly (or any pepper jelly)

Section 2 rolls, brush with butter, fold and roll with rolling pin to 5-inch square. Place Gouda cheese on top of dough, cover with 2 rolls prepared in same manner. Seal edges with fork dipped in flour. Brush with egg glaze. Bake on cookie sheet at 450 degrees until browned, about 10-15 minutes. Turn oven off. Spoon slightly warmed jelly over top of Wellington. Set in oven 5-10 minutes. Serve warm with crackers. Serves 10-12.

TIP! Always read labels and expiration dates on cheeses before purchasing. There's a difference between "aged" and "old."

SAUSAGE/CHEESE BALLS

Mix with hands in large bowl 1 pound sausage, 1 pound grated cheese and 2 cups biscuit mix. Shape into balls. Bake 25-30 minutes in 350-degree oven. These freeze well.

TINY HEAVENLY CHEESECAKES

PASTRY:
1 cup butter
1 (8-ounce) package cream cheese
2 cups flour
¼ teaspoon salt

Cream together the butter and cream cheese; add flour and salt and mix well. Shape into 24 small balls. Press each against sides and bottom of lightly greased miniature cupcake tins.

FILLING:
1 (6-ounce) package cream cheese, softened
2½ tablespoons sugar
1 teaspoon vanilla
1 egg

Mix together cream cheese, sugar, vanilla and egg. Spoon into pastry cups. Bake in 350-degree oven about 20 minutes. Cool. Just before serving, spread top of each with sour cream and dot with a little jam or fruit, if desired. Makes 24. These freeze well.

EASY CHEESY COCKTAIL SUGGESTIONS

Cream cheese with deviled ham, mustard and dash of Angostura bitters.
Cream cheese with chopped dill pickle.
Cream cheese, chopped watercress, touch of horseradish.
Cream cheese, finely chopped chutney, small amount of curry powder.
Cream cheese and horseradish.
Cream cheese, caviar and onion juice.
Cream cheese with chives and dash of Worcestershire.
Cream cheese, anchovy paste and a touch of grated onion.
Cream cheese covered with Pickapepper Sauce.
Cream cheese mixed with a jar of finely cut dried beef.
Cream cheese covered with hot pepper jelly.
Raw mushroom caps filled with cream cheese and a little horseradish and milk or cream.
Roquefort cheese moistened with Port wine.
Pimento cheese flavored with A-1 Sauce and a dash of onion salt or grated onion.
Jar of Old English sharp cheese mixed with jar of Bleu cheese.
Roquefort cheese (3 ounces) blended with 3 tablespoons each red wine (or sherry) and melted butter. Chill.
Cheddar cheese cubes marinated in port or sherry wine.
A roll of garlic cheese blended with a can of cream of mushroom soup. Serve warm in chafing dish with crackers or toast.
One pound Velveeta mixed with one can Rotel tomatoes and green chilies, served warm in chafing dish with big Fritoes or Doritoes.
One can Cheddar cheese soup mixed with one can Rotel tomatoes and green chilies.
Assorted cheese tray with garnishes of apples slices and bunches of grapes.

The Country Mouse Takes a Trip

The Country Mouse loves to travel.
Oh! The stories she tells . . . there are several.

To dine on cheeses of the very best
Is her requirement for a trip of success.

A recipe of cheese is her souvenir
A collection of her favorites are presented here.

ACROPOLIS SALAD

1 head of lettuce
½ pound Feta cheese (or Bleu)
4 large tomatoes
¼ pound black olives
1 small cucumber
1 large onion
Salt and pepper to taste
Anchovies, if desired

Wash and dry the lettuce thoroughly. Break up and put into a bowl. Break the Feta cheese into bite-sized pieces and put on top of lettuce. Quarter tomatoes and put on top of cheese along with the black olives. Peel and slice the cucumber and onion. Lay on top of tomatoes. Season generously with salt and pepper. Place anchovies on top. Serves 6.

GREEK DRESSING:
½ cup olive or salad oil   1/3 cup red wine vinegar

Combine the oil and vinegar and pour over salad just before serving.

NACHO TACO SALAD

1 large onion, chopped
1 pound ground meat
1 (1¼-ounces) package Taco Seasoning Mix
1 (15-ounce) can kidney beans, drained
Salt and pepper to taste
1 (8-ounce) package Nacho Tortillas
Shredded lettuce
Chopped tomatoes
Shredded sharp Cheddar cheese
Taco Sauce

In a large skillet, brown onions and ground meat. Drain; add seasoning mix and ¾ cup water. Then add kidney beans, salt and pepper. Simmer 15 minutes, stirring occasionally.

Place a handful of tortillas on a luncheon plate. Top with shredded lettuce, tomatoes, meat mixture and lastly cover with lots of sharp Cheddar cheese. Offer hot or mild Taco sauce and serve with crackers. Great Sunday night supper!

ROMANO SALAD DRESSING

8 ounces finely ground Romano cheese
1 pint salad oil
Juice of 2 lemons
Juice of 3 cloves of garlic

Shake all ingredients in a quart jar. Dressing will keep indefinitely in refrigerator. Especially good tossed with lettuce, water cress, and parsley leaves. Salt and pepper greens as desired before adding dressing.

ITALIAN MOZZARELLA LOAF

1 long loaf Italian bread
  with sesame seeds
½ cup salad olives, chopped

1 (16-ounce) package Mozzarella cheese, sliced
1½ teaspoons oregano

Preheat oven to 400 degrees. Cut bread in half lengthwise. Place cheese slices and olives on bottom bread slice. Cover with top.

Place bread on foil on cookie sheet and bake about 15 minutes or until cheese is melted. Sprinkle loaf with oregano. Slice and serve immediately. Try half Mozzarella and half Provolone.

TIP! As a rule, don't freeze cheese. Its texture may change. Shredded cheese freezes okay if used in cooking.

MOZZARELLA STICKS

¼ cup butter
½ cup flour
1½ cups milk, heated
1¼ cups shredded Mozza-
  rella cheese

1½ tablespoons horseradish
1 beef boullion cube
Oil for deep frying
1 fresh loaf Earth Grain very
  thin sandwich bread

Melt butter in medium saucepan over medium-high heat. Add flour and whisk until smooth. Slowly stir in milk. Add cheese, horseradish and bouillon cube and blend well. Reduce heat to low and cook 10 minutes. Remove from heat and cool.

Heat oil to 350 degrees. Remove crust from bread and roll flat with rolling pin or glass. Spread mixture evenly over bread slices. Roll each slice tightly. Fry in batches until golden brown on all sides. Drain on paper towels. Serve hot.

QUICHE LORRAINE

6-8 slices bacon
1 (8-inch) pastry shell,
  preferably puff pastry
1 cup (4 ounces) Gruyere
  or Swiss cheese, sliced

3 large eggs
1¼-1½ cups heavy cream
¼ teaspoon salt
Pinch of pepper and nutmeg
1-2 tablespoons butter

Cut bacon into ¼-inch pieces, brown and drain. Partially cook pastry shell (about 6 minutes in preheated 450-degree oven). Spread bacon bits on bottom of pastry shell alternately with cheese. Beat eggs, cream and seasonings well and pour into shell. Dot with butter. Bake at 375 degrees in upper third of oven 25-30 minutes until puffed and browned. Serve warm or cold.

BOURSIN CHEESE QUICHE

1 (9-inch) unbaked pie shell
1 cup shredded Swiss cheese
¼ cup chopped green onions,
  tops and stems
¼ cup chopped ripe olives

1 small tomato, diced
3 eggs
½ cup whipping cream
1 (5-ounce) package Boursin
  spice cheese

Preheat oven to 375 degrees. Sprinkle ¾ cup Swiss cheese on bottom of pastry. Sprinkle green olives and tomato over cheese.

In a medium bowl, mix eggs, cream and Boursin cheese; pour over vegetables. Sprinkle with remaining ¼ cup Swiss cheese. Bake on bottom shelf of oven 35 minutes or until puffed and golden brown. Let stand 5 minutes before cutting into wedges. Serves 8. Exquisite!

ALMOND FETTUCCINE

8 ounces thin egg noodles
¼ cup butter or oleo
1 cup (4 ounces) grated
  Parmesan cheese
¾ cup blanched, slivered
  almonds, toasted

½ cup whipped cream
2 tablespoons sliced green
  onions
Salt to taste
Pepper to taste

Cook noodles in boiling, salted water in a large saucepan as package directs. Turn into colander to drain. In the same pan, melt butter; stir in noodles. Heat and gently toss 2 minutes. Add remaining ingredients. Toss lightly to mix. Serves 4.

CHILI CORN CASSEROLE

2 cups fresh corn
½ cup butter, melted
2 eggs
1 cup sour cream
½ cup cornmeal
1 (4-ounce) can chopped green
 chili peppers
1½ teaspoons salt
1 cup diced Monterey Jack
 cheese

Preheat oven to 350 degrees. Generously butter a 2-quart casserole. Puree 1 cup corn with butter and eggs in blender. Mix remaining ingredients in bowl. Add pureed mixture and blend well. Pour into prepared dish. Bake uncovered 50-60 minutes.

GRECIAN ONE-DISH MEAL

1 cup brown rice, uncooked
2 tablespoons salad oil
2 medium onions, chopped
 finely
1 clove garlic, minced
Salt to taste
1 package frozen, chopped
 spinach, thawed
1 medium tomato, chopped
1 tablespoon lemon juice
1 cup (4 ounces) shredded
 Swiss cheese

Cook rice according to package directions (yields 4 cups of cooked rice). Meanwhile, heat oil in 10-inch skillet. Add onions and garlic. Cook until onion is tender. Add spinach and salt; stir and cook until spinach is tender, about 5 minutes. Stir in hot cooked rice, tomato and lemon juice. Sprinkle with cheese. Cover; let stand about 5 minutes so cheese can melt.

MICROWAVE ZUCCHINI MOZZARELLA

1½ pounds zucchini, sliced
¼ cup water
½ teaspoon salt
4 ounces Mozzarella slices
1 (4-ounce) can tomato sauce
¼ teaspoon Italian seasoning
Parmesan cheese

Place zucchini and water in a 3-quart casserole. Cover with waxed paper. Cook on High 15 minutes. Stir once during cooking time. Drain. Add salt.

Place slices of cheese over drained zucchini. Pour tomato sauce and seasoning over cheese and top with Parmesan cheese. Cook on High 3 minutes. Serves 6.

CRUSTY TACO SQUARES

1 pound ground beef
½ cup chopped onion
1 envelope taco seasoning mix
1 (16-ounce) can refried beans
1 (8-ounce) can tomato sauce
2 cans crescent dinner rolls
1 tablespoon oil
1/3 cup cornmeal
1 cup (4 ounces) shredded Cheddar cheese
1 cup (4 ounces) Monterey Jack cheese
2 cups shredded lettuce
1 cup chopped tomatoes
Taco sauce

Heat oven to 375 degrees. Brown meat and onions in skillet; drain. Stir in taco seasoning mix, beans and tomato sauce. Simmer 5 minutes.

Unroll dough into 4 long rectangles. Place in ungreased 15x10-inch jelly roll pan; press over bottom and 1 inch up sides to form crust. Brush dough with oil; sprinkle with cornmeal. Spoon hot meat mixture over crust. Bake 25-30 minutes or until crust is golden brown. Sprinkle with cheeses. Return to oven until cheese is melted, about 1-2 minutes. Cut into squares. Top with lettuce, tomatoes and taco sauce, as desired. Serves 8.

TIP! When broiling a dish topped with cheese, place the pan so that the cheese is several inches below the heat source. Broil just until the cheese melts.

ITALIAN SAUSAGE PIZZA

1 pound mild Italian sausage
1 cup chopped onion
1 cup chopped green pepper
1 (4-ounce) can mushroom stems and pieces, drained
1 (8-ounce) can tomato sauce
½ cup water
1 package hot roll mix
2½ cups (10 ounces) shredded Monterey Jack cheese

Heat oven to 425 degrees. Grease 15x10-inch jellyroll pan. Remove casing from sausage. In large skillet, brown sliced sausage with onion and green pepper; cook until vegetables are just tender. Drain; stir in mushrooms. Remove from heat.

In small saucepan, heat ½ cup tomato sauce and water until warm. Reserve remaining tomato sauce for topping. In large bowl, dissolve yeast from hot roll mix in warm tomato sauce and water. Stir in hot roll mix flour mixture; blend well. With greased fingers, press out dough in prepared pan forming rim around edge. Spread reserved tomato sauce over dough; sprinkle with cheese. Layer prepared sausage and vegetable mixture over cheese. Bake at 425 degrees 20-25 minutes or until crust is golden brown. Serves 6.

LA BELLA LASAGNE

2 tablespoons oleo
½ cup minced onion
1 pound lean ground beef
2 cloves garlic, minced
1 teaspoon oregano
¼ teaspoon parsley flakes
Salt and pepper to taste

2 tablespoons grated cheese
 (Parmesan and Romano)
1 (No. 2) can tomatoes
1 (8-ounce) can tomato sauce
½ (12-ounce) box lasagne
1 pound Mozzarella cheese,
 sliced

Saute onions in oleo. Add next 8 ingredients. Simmer covered ½ hour. Meanwhile, cook lasagne noodles. Rinse and drain. Layer in 9x13-inch baking dish, 1/3 meat mixture, lasagne noodles, Mozzarella cheese, etc. Bake at 350 degrees 45 minutes.

BEEF BURGUNDY STROGANOFF

4 pounds top round
3 tablespoons butter or oleo
1 onion, chopped
1 (10¼-ounce) can cream
 of mushroom soup
1 cup grated Cheddar

1 cup Burgundy
1 teaspoon crushed garlic
¼ teaspoon each: thyme, basil,
 and marjoram
Mushrooms, if desired
1 cup sour cream

Cut meat into thin strips and brown in butter. Remove meat and brown onion. Put meat and onion in large casserole. Add remaining ingredients except sour cream. Bake covered at 325 degrees for 2 hours. Stir in sour cream and bake 20 minutes more. Serve over rice, wild rice or noodles. Serves 8.

VITELLO ALLA PIEMONTSSE
(Piedmont Veal Cutlets)

¼ cup butter
2 tablespoons olive oil
1½ pounds veal cutlets, thinly
 sliced
2/3 cup dry white wine
1 teaspoon salt

½ teaspoon crushed oregano
½ teaspoon crushed basil
1 tablespoon dried parsley
Dash freshly ground pepper
6-8 ounces Provolone cheese,
 cut into 1-inch strips

Heat butter and oil in large skillet; add veal cutlets and brown. Stir in wine, salt, oregano, basil, parsley and pepper. Cook over low heat 15 minutes; baste frequently. Place cooked cutlets in a shallow baking pan; pour sauce over all. Put Provolone strips over each cutlet in a basket weave. Bake until cheese melts in preheated 350-degree oven. Serves 6.

PETITS CHOUX AU GRUYERE
(Little Cheese Puffs)

1 cup water
1 stick butter
1 teaspoon salt
1/8 teaspoon pepper
Dash nutmeg

1 cup flour, sifted
4 eggs
1 cup (4 ounces) grated Gruyere or Swiss cheese

Bring water to boil in saucepan with butter and seasonings untill butter has melted. Take off heat. Add flour all at once, beating vigorously with a wooden spoon until well blended. Return to medium high heat and continue beating 1-2 minutes until mixture leaves sides of pan and forms a mass. Take off heat again, make a well in center and break egg into it. Beat till absorbed. Repeat with each egg. Add cheese and blend well.

Mound by heaping teaspoonsful 1-2 inches apart on buttered baking sheets. Bake at 425 degrees 20 minutes. The choux should be golden on top. Makes 4-5 dozen. These freeze well.

TIP! Grated, shredded or diced cheese to be used in casseroles, sauces, or other cooked dishes should be added to other ingredients gradually in small amounts. Distribute it evenly.

MEXICAN CHEESE CASSEROLE

1 (4-ounce) can green chilies
1 pound Monterey Jack cheese, grated
1 pound Cheddar cheese, grated
4 egg whites, stiffly beaten

2/3 cup evaporated milk
1 tablespoon flour
½ teaspoon salt
¼ teaspoon pepper
Sliced tomatoes for top

Chop chilies in large bowl. Combine cheeses and chilies and place in 9x13-inch buttered casserole. In small bowl, combine egg yolks, milk, flour, salt and pepper. Fold in beaten egg whites. Pour on top of cheese and chilies in casserole, and push with a fork. Bake at 250 degrees 30 minutes. Remove from oven and place tomatoes on top. Bake another 30 minutes. Serve with green salad and French bread. Serves 6-8.

HEAVENLY KAHLUA CHEESECAKE

BOTTOM:

1¼ cups graham cracker
  crumbs
¼ cup sugar
¼ cup cocoa
1/3 cup butter or margarine,
  softened

Preheat oven to 325 degrees. Combine and mix all ingredients well. Firmly press mixture into bottom of a 9-inch springform pan. Bake 5 minutes; cool.

MIDDLE:

2 (8-ounce) packages cream
  cheese, softened
¾ cup sugar
1/3 cup cocoa
2 eggs
¼ cup strong coffee
¼ cup Kahlua or other coffee-
  flavored liqueur

Adjust oven to 375 degrees. Beat cream cheese with mixer till light and fluffy; gradually add sugar, mixing well. Beat in cocoa. Add eggs, one at a time, beating well after each addition. Stir in next 3 ingredients. Pour into prepared pan. Bake 25 minutes. (Filling will be soft but will firm up as cake stands.)

TOPPING:

1 cup sour cream
2 tablespoons sugar
1 teaspoon vanilla
6-8 chocolate curls (optional)

Adjust oven to 425 degrees. Combine all and spread over hot cheesecake. Bake 5-7 minutes. Let cool to room temperature on a wire rack; chill 8 hours or overnight.
  To serve, remove sides of springform pan. Garnish by placing 3 chocolate curls in center of cheesecake. Gently break remaining curls and sprinkle over top. Serves 10-12.

CAMEMBERT A LA RITZ

Camembert (4½-ounce round)
¼ cup finely chopped celery
¼ cup grated pared apple
¼ cup chopped walnuts

Remove top crust of Camembert and scoop out cheese leaving shell intact. (Shell is edible.) Cut Camembert into small cubes. In bowl, place apple, celery, walnuts and Camembert. Mix lightly with fork until blended. Pile mixture into empty Camembert shell. Serve at room temperature with bland crackers. A real delight!

HOT BUTTERED BRIE

1 (4½-ounce) round ripened Brie
1 tablespoon butter, softened
¼ cup slivered almonds, lightly toasted

Carefully cut top crust of Brie off with knife. Place cheese in an oven-proof serving dish. Spread top of cheese with softened butter. Add slivered almonds on top. Cover and bake at 325 degrees 15 minutes or until cheese is soft and creamy. Serve with assorted crackers, preferably bland, and green grapes or slices of pear. (Crust is edible.)

TIP! When selecting a delicate, not-long-keeping, soft-ripening cheese such as Brie, check the coloring. Is the rind uniformly white? Also check the odor; it should not be strong or ammoniacal. Is the center yielding when touched? It should be.

CHEESE TRUFFLES

¼ pound butter
½ cup grated Gouda or Edam cheese
1/8 teaspoon pepper
¼ teaspoon Beau Monde
¼ teaspoon paprika
1 cup stale pumpernickel or rye bread crumbs

Soften butter and beat till smooth, then mix in cheese and seasonings. Shape into olive-sized balls with a warm teaspoon, and roll each ball in the bread crumbs. Chill several hours before serving. Makes about 60 balls.

The Country Mouse Goes to the Church Bazaar

In the little church just round the bend,
The Ladies Auxiliary is at it again.

The church mouse has been chairman for many a year
And the bazaar's reputation has no peer.

You won't want to miss, I've heard it said,
Their little cheese crackers and special cheese bread.

APPLE CREAM CHEESE COFFEE CAKE

CAKE:
3 cups flour
1 cup sugar
4 teaspoons baking powder
1 teaspoon salt
1 1/3 cups milk
2/3 cup butter or oleo, melted
2 teaspoons vanilla
3 eggs

Heat oven to 375 degrees. Grease and flour 13x9-inch cake pan. Lightly spoon flour into measuring cup; level off. In large bowl, combine all ingredients in order given. Blend well. Pour into prepared pan.

FILLING:
1 (8-ounce) package cream cheese, softened
2 cups chopped pared apples
½ cup sugar
1 teaspoon cardamon
1 tablespoon flour
2 tablespoons butter or oleo, softened

In large bowl, combine all ingredients; mix well. Sprinkle mixture over batter; swirl gently with spatula.

TOPPING:
½ teaspoon cinnamon
1 tablespoon sugar
½ cup chopped nuts

In small bowl, combine all topping ingredients and sprinkle over cake. Bake at 375 degrees 40-50 minutes or until golden brown and toothpick inserted in center comes out clean. If desired, top with whipped cream. A moist, rich cake with a spicy, apple flavor! Serves 15.

EASTER MORNING COFFEE CAKE

1 (3-ounce) package cream cheese
4 tablespoons butter or oleo
2 cups biscuit mix
1/3 cup milk
½ cup strawberry preserves
1 cup sifted powdered sugar
1-2 tablespoons milk
½ teaspoon vanilla

Cut cream cheese and butter into biscuit mix till crumbly. Blend in 1/3 cup milk. Turn onto floured surface; knead 8-10 times. On waxed paper, roll dough to 12x8-inch rectangle. Turn onto greased baking sheet; remove paper. Spread preserves down center of dough. Make 2½-inch cuts at 1-inch intervals on long sides. Fold strips over filling. Bake in 425-degree oven 12-15 minutes. Combine sugar, remaining milk and vanilla and drizzle atop. Serves 6-8.

POLKA DOT DANISH ROLLS

2 (3-ounce packages cream cheese, softened
¼ cup sugar
2 tablespoons cherry juice
2 (8-ounce) cans crescent dinner rolls
4 Maraschino cherries, halved
½ cup powdered sugar

Heat oven to 375 degrees. In small bowl, blend cheese, sugar and 1 tablespoon juice until smooth. Separate 2 cans of dough into 8 rectangles; firmly press perforations to seal. Spread about 2 tablespoons cheese mixture on each rectangle. Starting at longer side, roll up, pressing edges to seal. Gently stretch each roll to about 11 inches. On ungreased cookie sheet, coil dough loosely into spiral shape with seam on inside of each roll, tucking end under and pinching to seal. Gently press cherry half into top of each. Bake 23-27 minutes or until deep golden brown. Cool.

In small bowl, combine powdered sugar and 1 tablespoon cherry juice; mix till smooth. If needed, add water a drop at a time to make desired consistency. Drizzle over warm rolls. Refrigerate leftovers. Pretty and good! Serves 8.

TIP! Cream cheese and Neufchatal will blend more flavorfully with other ingredients if they are softened slightly (brought to room temperature) before cooking.

HIDDEN DELIGHT MUFFINS

1 package carrot nut quick bread mix
¾ cup water
½ cup crushed pineapple, drained
½ cup golden raisins
1 egg, slightly beaten
1 (3-ounce) package cream cheese, cut into 12 cubes
2 tablespoons melted butter or margarine
Sugar

Heat oven to 400 degrees. Line muffin cups with paper liners. In large bowl, combine mix, water, pineapple, raisins and eggs. Stir just until dry particles are moistened. Fill prepared muffin cups half full; place one cream cheese cube on top of batter in each muffin cup; top each with 1 teaspoon remaining batter.

Bake 20-25 minutes or until top springs back when lightly touched. Cool 5 minutes; remove from pan. Brush with melted margarine; sprinkle lightly with sugar. Serve warm. Refrigerate leftovers. Makes 12 muffins.

CHEESAPPLE DUMPLINGS

4 small to medium-size
  baking apples
2 tablespoons brown sugar
2 tablespoons softened butter
1 tablespoon chopped raisins
1 tablespoon chopped walnuts
  (may use pecans)
1 recipe chilled cheese dough
1 egg beaten

Preheat oven to 425 degrees. Peel and core apples. Combine brown sugar, butter, raisins and walnuts. Stuff core of apples with mixture. Roll out chilled cheese dough to 1/8-inch thickness. Cut four 7-inch squares of dough. Wrap each apple in a square of dough by bringing corners of dough together on top of apple. Press edges together. Make pastry decorations with any leftover dough, then brush with beaten egg. Bake 25 minutes. Serve warm.

CHEESE DOUGH:

1½ cups flour
½ cup butter, softened
1/8 teaspoon salt
½ cup (2 ounces) finely
  shredded Cheddar cheese
¼ cup water

Combine flour, butter and salt. Using a pastry cutter or two knives, cut butter into flour until mixture resembles coarse crumbs. Add shredded cheese. Sprinkle with water while stirring. Form into a ball; chill while preparing apples. This is a delicious crust for dumplings or your favorite apple pie.

APRICOT NIBBLE BREAD

2 (3-ounce) packages cream
  cheese, softened
1/3 cup sugar
1 tablespoon flour
1 egg
1 teaspoon grated orange peel
1 slightly beaten egg
½ cup orange juice
½ cup water
1 (17-ounce) package apricot-
  nut quick bread mix

Combine cream cheese, sugar and flour; beat in the first egg and the orange peel. Set mixture aside. Combine the slightly beaten egg, the orange juice and water. Add quick bread mix, stirring till moistened. Turn 2/3 of the apricot batter into greased and floured loaf pan. Pour cheese mixture over top; spoon on remaining batter. Bake in 350-degree oven 1 hour. Cool 10 minutes; remove from pan. Cool. Wrap in foil; refrigerate. Good served at morning bridge with mixture of cream cheese and apricot preserves spread on top.

TIPSY BREAD

3 cups flour
1 (1-ounce) package dry
  yeast
½ cup dry white wine
½ cup butter or margarine

2 teaspoons sugar
1 teaspoon salt
3 eggs
1 cup (4 ounces) cubed Monterey Jack cheese

In large mixer bowl, combine 1½ cups flour and the yeast. In saucepan, heat wine, butter, sugar and salt till just warm (115-120 degrees), stirring constantly until butter almost melts. Add to dry mixture in mixer bowl. Add eggs. Beat at low speed of electric mixer ½ minute, scraping sides of bowl constantly. Beat 3 minutes at high speed. By hand, stir in cheese and enough remaining flour to make a soft dough. Turn out onto lightly floured surface. Knead till smooth and elastic. Place in lightly greased bowl, turning once to grease surface. Cover and let rise in warm place till double, about 1½ hours.

Punch dough down; cover and let rest 10 minutes. Shape into 8-inch round loaf. Place in a greased 9-inch pie plate; cover and let rise in warm place till double (about 40 minutes). Bake in 375-degree oven about 40 minutes, covering with foil after the first 20 minutes of baking.

TIP! When using shredded cheese to prepare baked boods, first bring the cheese to room temperature, so that it will blend more evenly in the batter or dough.

MARTHA'S CHEESE STRAWS

½ pound sharp Cheddar
  cheese
1 stick oleo, softened

1½ cups flour
½ teaspoon salt
Cayenne pepper to taste

Grate cheese. Mix all together well. Put in a cookie press (star shape) or make a roll. Refriferate until hard and slice. Bake at 325 degrees about 15 minutes. Super!

SESAME CHEESE STRAWS

Add 1 (2¼-ounce) jar sesame seeds toasted in heavy skillet 20 minutes over low heat (stir often) to above recipe.

CHEESE CRACKER CRISPIES

2 cups flour
2 cups sharp Cheddar cheese, grated, room temperature
2 cups rice krispies
2 sticks oleo, softened
1 teaspoon salt or ½ teaspoon garlic salt
1 teaspoon Tabasco or 1 teaspoon cayenne pepper
1 teaspoon Worcestershire

Mix ingredients well. Form into small balls, place on ungreased cookie sheet and press with fork. Bake at 300 degrees until golden brown. Makes 90.

TIP! Cheese should be kept cool, about 35-38 degrees (bottom shelf of your refrigerator). Wrap in air-tight baggies or plastic wrap, and make sure to squeeze out as much air as possible before sealing.

BISHOP'S SWISS BEER BREAD

1½ cups beer
½ cup water
2 tablespoons sugar
3 teaspoons salt
2 tablespoons butter or oleo
1 (8-ounce) package process Swiss cheese
5 cups flour
2 (1-ounce) packages active dry yeast

In large saucepan, heat beer, water, sugar, salt, butter and cheese until very warm. Cheese need not melt completely. In large bowl, combine 2 cups lightly measured flour with yeast; add warm cheese mixture. Beat 3 minutes at medium speed. By hand, gradually stir in remaining 3 cups flour to make a fairly stiff dough. Knead on lightly floured surface until smooth and elastic, about 5 minutes. Place in greased bowl, turning to grease top. Cover; let rise in warm place until light and doubled in size, 45-60 minutes.

Generously grease (not oil) bottom and sides of 2 loaf pans. Punch dough down; divide in half and shape into two 11x5 rectangles. Cut each rectangle into 3 long strips, leaving strips joined at one end. Braid; place in greased pans. Cover; let rise in warm place until light and doubled in size, 45-60 minutes.

Heat oven to 350 degrees. Bake 40-45 minutes or until golden brown and loaf sounds hollow when lightly tapped. Remove from pan immediately; cool completely. Great flavor!

GOOD-FOR-THE-SOUL CHEESE BREAD

7½ cups unsifted flour
½ cup sugar
1 tablespoon salt
2 (1-ounce) packages yeast
2 cups water

2/3 cup milk
3 cups (12 ounces) shredded sharp Cheddar cheese
Melted margarine

Combine 2½ cups flour, sugar, salt and undissolved yeast. Heat water and milk over low heat until liquids are 120-130 degrees. Add to dry ingredients; beat 2 minutes at medium speed, scraping bowl occasionally. Add cheese and ½ cup flour. Beat at high speed 2 minutes. Stir in enough flour to make a stiff dough. Turn onto floured board. Knead about 8-10 minutes. Place in greased bowl; grease top. Cover and let rise until doubled, about 1 hour.

Punch dough down; turn onto floured board. Cover, let rest for 15 minutes. Divide in half and shape into loaves. Place in 2 greased loaf pans. Cover; let rise until doubled, about 1 hour.

Bake on lowest rack position at 375 degrees about 40 minutes, or until done. Remove from pans and cool. Brush with melted margarine. Wonderful toasted!

CHEESY BUNS

1 package dry yeast
2 cups flour, divided
1 (5-ounce) jar sharp process cheese spread
½ cup water

¼ cup shortening
2 tablespoons sugar
¾ teaspoon salt
1 egg, beaten

Combine yeast and 1 cup flour in a medium mixing bowl; set aside. Combine cheese spread, water, shortening, sugar and salt in a small saucepan. Heat to 105-115 degrees, stirring constantly. Add cheese mixture and egg to yeast mixture; beat half a minute on low speed of electric mixer, scraping sides of bowl. Beat 3 minutes on high. Stir in remaining flour.

Turn out on a lightly floured surface, and knead 1-2 minutes. Shape dough into 1½-inch balls. Place in well-greased muffin cups. Let rise in a warm place (85 degrees) free from drafts, 1½ hours, or until doubled in bulk. Bake at 350 degrees for 12-18 minutes till brown. Yields 1 dozen delicious buns!

DILLY-LICIOUS BREAD

2 packages dry yeast
½ cup warm water
2 tablespoons plus 2 teaspoons sugar, divided
2 cups cream-style cottage cheese
2 tablespoons dried dillweed
2 tablespoons finely chopped onion
1 teaspoon baking powder
1 teaspoon salt
2 eggs, beaten
4½ cups flour
Melted butter

Dissolve yeast in warm water (105-115 degrees) in a large bowl; stir in 2 teaspoons sugar. Set aside.

In a small mixing bowl, combine next 6 ingredients and remaining sugar; add to yeast mixture, mixing well. Gradually add flour, stirring well. Turn dough out onto a floured surface, knead till smooth and elastic, about 8-10 minutes (dough will be sticky). Place in a well-greased bowl, turning to grease top. Cover and let rise in a warm place free from drafts, about 1 hour or until double in bulk.

Punch dough down and divide in half. Shape each half into a loaf. Place in 2 well-greased loaf pans. Cover and let rise in a warm place about 40 minutes or until doubled in bulk. Bake at 350 degrees 30-35 minutes or until loaves sound hollow when tapped. Remove from pans and brush with melted butter. Great flavor!

TIP! When cooking with cheese, generally keep the heat low. Cheese needs just enough heat to allow it to melt and blend well with other ingredients. High heat or long cooking causes fat separation, making cheese tough and stringy. Dry heat, prolonged baking, or high temps will produce a leathery texture.

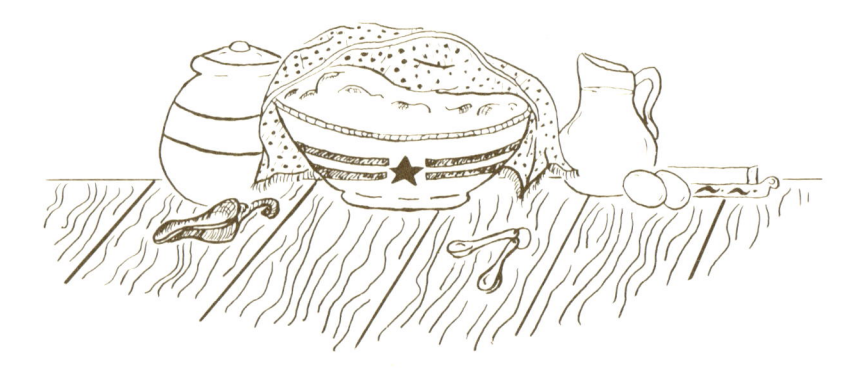

SUNSHINE BARS

BASE:
1 cup flour
½ cup sugar
½ cup butter or margarine, softened

FILLING:
2 tablespoons sugar
1 (8-ounce) package cream cheese, softened
2 tablespoons milk
1 teaspoon vanilla
1 egg
1 (20-ounce) can crushed pineapple, drained

TOPPING:
1 cup coconut
1 tablespoon butter, melted

Heat oven to 350 degrees. Mix all base ingredients together well till crumbly. Press in bottom of ungreased 13x9-inch pan. Bake 10-15 minutes until golden.

In small bowl, beat sugar, cream cheese, milk, vanilla and egg at medium speed for 3 minutes until smooth; stir in drained pineapple. Pour over partially baked crust.

Combine coconut and melted butter or margarine; sprinkle over filling. Return to oven and bake 15-20 minutes or until filling is set and coconut is golden brown. Cool completely; cut into bars. Makes 36 bars. Store in refrigerator; remove 20 minutes before cutting.

MINTED BROWNIES

½ pound butter
2 cups sugar
4 eggs
4 squares unsweetened chocolate, melted
1½ teaspoons vanilla
1½ cups sifted flour
1 (8-ounce) package cream cheese, softened
¼ cup sugar
2 tablespoons Creme de Menthe
1 egg, beaten

Cream butter and sugar. Add 1 egg at a time, beating well with a fork. Add melted chocolate and vanilla; fold in flour; mix well and set aside.

Preheat oven to 350 degrees. In separate bowl, combine cream cheese, ¼ cup sugar and Creme de Menthe. Blend well and add beaten egg; blend well again. Spread half the brownie mix in buttered, floured 9x13-inch pan. Cover with cream cheese mixture. Spoon on remaining brownie batter. Bake 35-40 minutes. Cut into 1½-inch squares. Makes 24. Delicious!

PARISH PECAN POUND CAKE

1½ cups chopped pecans
1½ cups butter, softened
1 (8-ounce) package cream
  cheese, softened
3 cups sugar
6 eggs
3 cups sifted cake flour
½ teaspoon salt
1½ teaspoons vanilla

Sprinkle ½ cup pecans in a greased, floured 10-inch tube pan; set aside. Cream butter and cream cheese; gradually add sugar, beating until light and fluffy. Add eggs, one at a time, beating well after each addition. Add flour and salt, stirring until well mixed. Stir in vanilla and remaining 1 cup pecans. Beat another minute. Pour batter into pan. Bake at 325 degrees 1½ hours or until wooden pick inserted in center comes out clean. Cool in pan 10 minutes; remove from pan and cool completely on rack.

Served with a colorful tray of sliced fruit and Gouda (or any kind of cheese) makes any get together a memorable occasion.

MYSTERY PECAN PIE

1 (8-ounce) package cream
  cheese, softened
1/3 cup sugar
½ teaspoon salt
1 teaspoon vanilla
1 egg
1¼ cups chopped pecans
1 (9-inch) pie shell, unbaked

TOPPING:
3 eggs
¼ cup sugar
1 cup light or dark corn syrup
1 teaspoon vanilla

Heat oven to 375 degrees. In small bowl, combine cream cheese, sugar, salt, vanilla and egg; beat at medium speed until well blended. Spread in bottom of pastry-lined pan. Sprinkle with pecans.

In small bowl, combine all topping ingredients; beat on medium speed just until blended. Gently pour over pecans. Bake 35-40 minutes or until center is firm to touch. Refrigerate leftovers. Serves 8.

CREAM CHEESE FROSTING

1 (8-ounce) package cream
  cheese, softened
1 stick butter, softened
1 teaspoon vanilla
1 (1-pound) box powdered
  sugar

Cream cheese and butter well and add vanilla. Beat in sugar a little at a time until of spreading consistency. Delicious on carrot cake, Italian cream cake, or your favorite.

The Country Mouse Has a Dinner Party

*Company is coming for dinner tonight.
The Country Mouse wants her menu just right.*

*She'll start with a fancy cheese hors d'oeuvre
Then a spectacular cheese entree she'll serve.*

*For dessert something scrumptious—cheesy and rich
Cheesecake or crepes—which would you pick?*

PORCUPINE BALL

Cut your favorite cheese into 3/4-inch cubes. Cut a slice from one end of an orange to make a firm base. Pierce the cheese cubes on a cocktail stick. Add a grape, cherry, mandarin segment or a piece of pineapple to each cube. Push the other end of the stick into the orange to form a "porcupine."

Instead of an orange, you may want to use a grapefruit or a red cabbage. Interesting to try several kinds of gourmet cheeses on your guests.

CAVIAR CREAM SUPREME

Mix a softened 3-ounce package of cream cheese with 2 tablespoons of sour cream, 3 finely chopped hard-cooked eggs, and a dash of paprika. Spread generously on dark pumpernickel bread or Melba toast and top with caviar. Serve with slices of lemon.

TIP! The classic way to serve cheese is with fruit and/or beverage such as wine, beer, ale, even cider or fruit-wine. The milder the cheese, the milder the beverage should be, and vice-versa. But there are no strict rules. Whatever you like is right!

ELEGANTE SWISS BROCCOLI SOUP

5½ cups whole milk
1 (10-ounce) package frozen chopped broccoli or 1½ cups chopped fresh broccoli
2 tablespoons chopped onion
2 tablespoons butter
1 tablespoon flour
2 cups (½ pound) shredded Swiss cheese
Salt to taste

Heat milk in large saucepan to simmering. Cook broccoli and onions in milk until tender. Melt butter in small saucepan. Stir in flour. Add butter-flour mixture to milk. Cook and stir 3 minutes. Remove from heat; add shredded cheese and salt. Stir until cheese is melted. Serve immediately. Delicious!

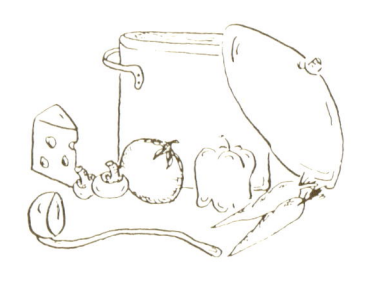

EDAM UP SOUP

1½ cups baby lima beans, cooked
8 strips lean bacon
½ cup chopped onion
½ cup chopped celery
½ cup flour
5 cups milk
2 cups (8 ounces) Edam (or Cheddar), shredded
Salt and freshly ground black pepper to taste
Dash of Cayenne pepper
¼ cup finely chopped parsley

Cook lima beans following dry or frozen package directions. If using canned beans, just drain and rinse. Set aside. Cut bacon into ½-inch pieces and saute lightly in 2-quart saucepan. When bacon is limp but not completely cooked, stir in onion and celery and continue to saute till onion is transparent. Sprinkle in flour and stir well to avoid lumps. Add milk slowly and continue stirring. Stir in beans and cook till mixture begins to thicken. Stir in cheese, salt, pepper and cayenne. Cook over low heat until the cheese has melted. Stir in parsley and serve. Serves 6-8.

CHEF'S THREE-CHEESE SALAD

1 small head iceberg lettuce
1 head Boston lettuce
¼ pound chicory or other greens
1 medium cucumber, sliced
1 sweet red onion, thinly sliced
2 tomatoes, cut into wedges
¼ pound hard salami, cut into thin strips
¼ pound ham, cut into strips
¼ pound chicken or turkey, cut into strips
¼ pound Swiss, cut into strips
¼ pound Colby, cut into strips
¼ pound Provolone, cut into strips
Green and black olives
3 hard-cooked eggs

Wash the salad greens and drain thoroughly. Tear into bite-sized pieces and toss together in a large salad bowl. Arrange the cucumber, onion, and tomato wedges on top of the greens. Alternate strips of meat, poultry, and cheeses around the bowl and decorate with olives. Garnish with hard-cooked egg wedges. Serves 8.

CHEF'S DRESSING:
1/3 cup red wine vinegar
½ cup olive oil or salad oil
1 garlic clove, finely minced
¼ teaspoon Dijon mustard
¼ teaspoon salt

Combine all ingredients and mix thoroughly. Pour dressing over salad just before serving.

CHEESE BACON DRESSING

¾ cup salad oil
¼ cup vinegar
¾ teaspoon salt
¼ teaspoon pepper
1 clove garlic, pressed
1/3 cup crisp crumbled bacon or imitation bacon bits
2/3 cup finely grated Cheddar cheese
Dash Worcestershire

Place all ingredients in pint jar. Cover and shake vigorously. Pour over chilled, sliced tomatoes.

ROQUEFORT CHEESE DRESSING

2 tablespoons mayonnaise
2 tablespoons sweet cream
3 tablespoons Roquefort
Freshly ground pepper
3 tablespoons oil (half olive, half salad oil)
1 tablespoon white wine vinegar
1 crushed clove of garlic

Combine ingredients and mix until creamy with electric mixer. Makes 1 quart. Bottle and store in refrigerator.

SOUTHERN ROQUEFORT CHEESE DRESSING

¾ pound Roquefort or 1 pound Bleu cheese
2 cups mayonnaise
1 cup sour cream
Juice of 1 lemon
1 small onion, grated

Thin mayonnaise with cream; add crumbled cheese and blend well. Stir in oil, vinegar and pepper to taste; mix well. Add garlic for flavor, but remove before pouring dressing over salad.

AMBROSIA CREAM SALAD

1 ounce unflavored gelatin
½ cup cold water
1 (15½-ounce) can unsweetened pineapple chunks
1/3 cup sugar
Juice of one lemon
2 (3-ounce) packages cream cheese, softened
1 orange, peeled, sectioned, and diced
½ cup flaked coconut
½ cup chopped pecans

Soften gelatin in water; let stand 5 minutes. Drain pineapple and add enough water to juice to make 1 cup. Heat to boiling; add gelatin mixture and stir until dissolved. Remove from heat; stir in sugar, lemon juice, and cream cheese, using a wire whisk to blend. Chill until gelatin is partially set; fold in pineapple, orange, coconut and pecans. Spoon into a lightly greased 1-quart mold; chill until firm. Unmold on lettuce leaves and garnish with lemon slices, if desired. Six simply delicious servings!

TOMATO ASPIC WITH BLEU CHEESE TOPPING

3 (1-ounce) envelopes unflavored gelatin
1 (46-ounce) can tomato juice, divided
2 tablespoons grated onion
½ teaspoon salt
1 cup chopped green pepper
1 cup chopped celery
Bleu Cheese Topping

Soften gelatin in 1½ cups tomato juice; heat to dissolve gelatin. While warm, add onion salt, and remaining tomato juice. Chill until slightly thickened; add green pepper and celery. Pour into a 9-cup mold; chill till firm. Serve with *Bleu Cheese Topping*. Serves 10-12.

BLEU CHEESE TOPPING:
1 (3-ounce) package cream cheese, softened
3 tablespoons milk
1 (3-ounce) package Bleu cheese, crumbled

Combine cream cheese and milk; blend well. Add Bleu cheese and beat till thick. Makes 1 cup. The Bleu Cheese really makes the aspic different and delicious!

ENGLISH PEA 'N CHEDDAR CHEESE SALAD

2 (16-ounce) cans small English peas, drained
3-4 stalks celery, finely cut
½ onion, grated
3-4 tablespoons pickle relish
2-4 dill pickles, grated
½ green pepper, finely cut
1 cup (4 ounces) Cheddar cheese, diced
¾-1 cup mayonnaise
Salt to taste

Mix all ingredients. Chill well. Serves 10. Delightful buffet dish.

SPINACH ELEGANTE

2 (10-ounce) packages frozen chopped spinach
4 slices bacon, cooked and crumbled
1 (6-ounce) can mushrooms, drained, chopped or sliced
¼ teaspoon dried marjoram, crushed
1 cup sour cream
½ cup (2 ounces) sharp Cheddar cheese, grated

Cook spinach according to the package directions; drain well. Spread on bottom of casserole dish, then bacon, mushrooms, pepper and marjoram. Bake at 325 degrees 15 minutes. Cover with sour cream and cheese. Bake 5 minutes until cheese melts.

CARROTS AU GRATIN

3 cups sliced carrots, cooked
1 (10¾-ounce) can cream of celery soup
1 cup (4 ounces) shredded Cheddar cheese

AU GRATIN TOPPING:
1 tablespoon margarine or butter, melted
¼ cup dry bread crumbs

Heat oven to 350 degrees. Butter a 1-quart casserole. In medium bowl, combine carrots, soup and cheese. Pour into prepared casserole. In a small bowl, combine bread crumbs and margarine. Sprinkle topping over carrots. Bake 25 minutes. Serves 6. Will make carrot lovers out of your children!

HEAVENLY POTATO CLOUDS

6 eggs, separated
1½ cups water
½ teaspoon garlic salt
1½ cups mashed potato flakes
½ cup grated Cheddar cheese
1 cup small curd cottage cheese
½ cup sour cream
¼ cup minced green onion
1 tablespoon minced parsley

Heat oven to 350 degrees. Lightly grease 2-quart casserole or 8 custard cups or ramekins. In small bowl, beat egg whites until stiff peaks form; set aside.

In medium saucepan, heat water and garlic salt to a rolling boil. Remove from heat; stir in potato flakes. Add cottage cheese, cheese, sour cream, onion, parsley and egg yolks. Mix well. Carefully fold in beaten egg whites. Lightly spoon into prepared baking dish. Bake at 350 degrees 1 hour or until puffed and golden brown. Serves 8. Light as a feather and lovely to serve!

MICROWAVE GARLIC CHEESE GRITS

½ cup grits
2 cups water
1/3 cup butter
2 eggs, well beaten
1 (6-ounce) roll garlic cheese, chopped

Bring water to boil in a 2-quart casserole. Add grits, cover with waxed paper and microwave on High 3 minutes. Add butter and stir in eggs slowly. Add chopped cheese and stir until melted. Microwave covered on Medium 8 minutes, turning 2 or 3 times. Let stand 5 minutes before serving.

DELICATE SWISS CHEESE GRITS

1 quart milk
6 tablespoons butter
1 cup 3-minute grits
Salt and pepper to taste

1 cup (4 ounces) grated natural Swiss cheese (aged)
1/3 cup freshly grated Parmesan cheese

Bring milk and 4 tablespoons butter to a slow boil, then stir in grits slowly. Stir often till mixture thickens. Put in large mixer bowl and beat with electric mixer till creamy, about 5 minutes. Add Swiss cheese, salt and pepper and mix with wooden spoon.

Pour into a greased 2-quart casserole. Dot with 2 tablespoons of butter and sprinkle with Parmesan. Bake at 375 degrees 35-40 minutes. Serves 6-8. The best!

FANCY FRENCH GREEN BEANS

2 tablespoons margarine or butter
3 tablespoons flour
1 cup sour cream
2 (16-ounce) cans French-style green beans, drained

1½ cups (6 ounces) shredded Swiss cheese
½ teaspoon salt
¼ teaspoon pepper
1 (3-ounce) can French fried onions

Heat oven to 350 degrees. In medium saucepan, melt margarine; blend in flour until smooth. Stir in sour cream. Cook over low heat until slightly thickened—do not boil. Add all remaining ingredients except French fried onions; toss gently. Pour into 1½-quart casserole. Bake at 350 degrees 25 minutes. Sprinkle with onions and bake 3-5 minutes longer. Serves 8.

PARMESAN PULL-APART BREAD

¼ cup margarine or butter, melted
1 clove garlic, minced or ¼ teaspoon garlic powder

½ teaspoon dry mustard
1 (10-ounce) can refrigerated flaky biscuits
¾ cup grated Parmesan cheese

Heat oven to 400 degrees. Combine melted margarine, garlic and dry mustard. Coat bottom of an 8 or 9-inch round cake pan with 1 tablespoon of the margarine mixture (reserve remainder for topping). Separate dough into 10 biscuits; cut each into 4 pieces. Arrange biscuit pieces evenly in prepared pan. Drizzle reserved margarine mixture over biscuit pieces; sprinkle with Parmesan cheese. Bake at 400 degrees for 12 to 17 minutes or until golden brown. Turn onto wire rack; invert onto serving place. Serve warm.

SPICY SPINACH-STUFFED SQUASH

4 yellow crookneck squash
2 (10-ounce) packages frozen
　chopped spinach
4 tablespoons butter
2 tablespoons flour
½ cup evaporated milk
½ teaspoon black pepper
¾ teaspoon celery salt
¾ teaspoon garlic powder
1 teaspoon Worcestershire
Dash red pepper
1 (6-ounce) roll Jalapeno cheese
1 cup tiny bread cubes sauteed
　in 2 tablespoons butter
Freshly grated Parmesan cheese

Wash squash and cut into halves. Place in boiling water for about 10 minutes until slightly tender, but not soft. Remove and take pulp from squash. (Use for another recipe, if desired.)

Cook spinach in unsalted water and drain well, reserving ½ cup of the liquid. Melt butter in saucepan, add flour and whisk in milk and reserved spinach liquid. Cook, stirring, until thickened and add seasonings. Cut up cheese and add to sauce to melt, then add spinach and bread cubes. Spoon mixture into squash shells and top with freshly grated Parmesan cheese. Put back into oven and heat thoroughly or until cheese melts. Serve immediately. Serves 8.

TIP! When topping a casserole, do not add the cheese until the very last minute. Allow it to cook only until the cheese melts.

BROCCOLI 'N RICE 'R NICE

1 stick butter or oleo
1 onion, finely chopped
1 rib celery, chopped
1 (10-ounce) package frozen
　chopped broccoli
1 (10¼-ounce) can cream
　of chicken soup, undiluted
1 cup (4 ounces) grated sharp
　Cheddar cheese
1½ cups cooked rice
Tabasco to taste
Salt and pepper to taste
½ cup (2 ounces) grated sharp
　Cheddar cheese

In a large skillet, saute onions and celery in butter until vegetables are clear. Cook broccoli according to package directions; drain well. Mix broccoli with soup and 1 cup cheese; add to celery and onions. Stir in cooked rice; season and mix well.

Pour into a greased 8x8x2-inch casserole and top with ½ cup cheese. Bake at 350 degrees 45 minutes. This can be mixed ahead and frozen. Serves 6.

FETTUCCINE MAGNIFICO

1 cup whipping cream
3 tablespoons real butter
1 (12-ounce) package
  fettuccine noodles
2/3 cup freshly grated
  Parmesan cheese
Salt to taste
Freshly ground pepper to taste
Pinch of nutmeg
2 tablespoons fresh parsley,
  chopped (optional)

Simmer 2/3 cup of the cream and all butter in large saucepan over medium heat until slightly thickened, a minute or two. Take off heat.

Drop fettuccine into boiling, salted water and cover the pot until the water returns to a boil. Lower heat and boil gently until noodles are al dente, about 8-10 minutes--they will cook a little more in the pan. Drain thoroughly and transfer to cream mixture. Over low heat, toss fettuccine, coating noodles with sauce. Add remainder of cream, grated cheese, and seasonings. Toss briefly until cream has thickened and noodles are well coated. Taste and correct for salt. Serve immediately with extra cheese. Magnifico!

FESTIVE CHICKEN WITH ASPARAGUS

6 chicken breasts, deboned
2 tablespoons flour
3 tablespoons salad oil
1/4 cup (1 ounce) Bleu cheese,
  crumbled
1/4 cup dry white wine
1 (10 1/4-ounce) can cream of
  chicken soup, undiluted
1/2 teaspoon salt
1/4 teaspoon pepper
1 pound asparagus or
  1 (15-ounce) can asparagus

On waxed paper, coat chicken breasts with flour. Preheat oven to 375 degrees. In 12-inch skillet over medium-high heat in hot salad oil, cook chicken pieces until lightly browned on all sides. Meanwhile, in shallow 3-quart casserole, mix well Bleu cheese, wine and undiluted cream of chicken soup and spoon mixture over chicken to coat it. Bake in oven 30 minutes.

To prepare asparagus, hold base of stalk firmly and bend stalk; end will break off at spot where it becomes tough to eat. Discard ends; trim scales, if stalks are gritty. Cut each asparagus spear crosswise in half; rinse under running cold water; drain.

Remove casserole from oven and arrange asparagus between chicken pieces. Cover casserole tightly with foil or lid and bake 30 minutes longer or until chicken is fork-tender and asparagus is tender-crisp. Serve in casserole. Serves 6.

JIM'S JELLY-ROLL MEATLOAF

1½ pounds lean ground beef
2 slices bread, crumbled
2 eggs, beaten

1 tablespoon Worcestershire
1 teaspoon garlic powder
1 teaspoon salt

FILLING:

1 (10-ounce) package frozen spinach, thawed and drained

2 teaspoons salt
½ pound shredded Mozzarella

SAUCE:

1 cup tomato sauce
1 teaspoon basil
1 teaspoon chopped parsley

1 teaspoon salt
1 teaspoon garlic powder
1 teaspoon oregano

TOPPING:

1 tablespoon Parmesan

½ pound shredded Mozzarella

Grind 2 slices of bread into crumbs. Add to ground meat. Stir in eggs, Worcestershire sauce, garlic powder and salt. Mix well. Flatten mixture into a 9x12-inch shape about ½-inch thick.

Spread drained, thawed spinach over meat. Sprinkle salt, then cheese over spinach. Starting at the longest side, roll up in jelly-roll fashion, pinching ends together when finished. Place in greased loaf pan. Bake at 350 degrees 45 minutes or until done.

Meanwhile, add basil, parsley, salt, garlic powder, and oregano to tomato sauce in saucepan. Bring to boil. Reduce and simmer while meat is cooking. Stir occasionally.

Drain meatloaf when done and carefully place it on ovenproof plate. Pour sauce over loaf. Sprinkle both cheeses on top and place back into oven long enough to melt cheese. Serves 8.

SWISS REUBEN PIE

1 unbaked 9-inch pastry shell
6 ounces thinly sliced corned beef, shredded
1 cup (4 ounces) shredded Swiss cheese
½ cup well-drained sauerkraut

2 tablespoons all-purpose flour
¼ teaspoon salt
Dash of ground nutmeg
2 eggs, beaten
1 cup Half-and-Half

Prick bottom and sides of pastry shell with a fork. Bake at 425 degrees for 7 minutes. Sprinkle corned beef in pastry shell; add cheese, and top with chopped sauerkraut. Combine remaining ingredients, mixing well. Pour over sauerkraut in pastry shell. Bake at 325 degrees 35-40 minutes or until set. Let pie stand 10 minutes before serving.

CHICKEN PARMICHEESA

*3 whole chicken breasts,
  split, boned and skinned*
2 eggs, slightly beaten
1 teaspoon salt
1/8 teaspoon pepper
¾ cup fine dry breadcrumbs
½ cup vegetable oil

1 (15-ounce) can tomato sauce
¼ teaspoon dried whole basil
1/8 teaspoon garlic powder
1 tablespoon butter or oleo
½ cup grated Parmesan cheese
*8 ounces Mozzarella cheese,
  thinly sliced, cut into triangles*

Place each chicken breast on a sheet of waxed paper. Flatten to ¼-inch thickness, using a meat mallet or rolling pin. Combine eggs, salt, and pepper. Dip chicken breasts into egg mixture, then roll each in breadcrumbs.

Brown chicken in hot oil in a large skillet; drain on paper towels. Place chicken in a lightly greased 13x9x2 baking dish. Drain oil from skillet. Combine tomato sauce, basil, and garlic powder in skillet. Bring to a boil, and simmer 10 minutes or until thickened. Stir in butter.

Pour mixture over chicken; sprinkle with Parmesan cheese. Cover and bake at 350 degrees 30 minutes. Uncover and arrange Mozzarella slices on top. Bake additional 10 minutes. Serves 6.

SEASHELL-PROVOLONE CASSEROLE

*3 medium onions, finely
  chopped*
¼ cup butter or oleo, melted
1½-2 pounds ground beef
*1 (15½-ounce) jar plain
  spaghetti sauce*
1 can (or 2 cups) tomatoes
*1 (16-ounce) can mushroom
  stems and pieces*

1 teaspoon garlic salt
*1 (8-ounce) package seashell
  macaroni*
*1 (8-ounce) package Provolone
  cheese, sliced*
3 cups sour cream
*1 cup (4 ounces) shredded
  Mozzarella cheese*

Saute onions in butter in a large skillet just until tender. Add ground beef; cook until browned, stirring to crumble meat; drain. Add spaghetti sauce, tomatoes, mushrooms, and garlic salt to meat mixture. Stir well and simmer 20 minutes.

Cook macaroni according to package directions, except reduce salt to 1½ teaspoons; drain. Place half of macaroni in a deep 4-quart greased casserole; layer with half of meat sauce, half of Provolone, and half of sour cream. Repeat layers and top with Mozzarella. Cover and bake at 350 degrees 30 minutes; uncover and bake another 15 minutes. Serves 12.

GOLDEN CHEESE BRAID

1/3 cup (3 ounces) shredded
  sharp natural Cheddar
1/3 cup whole kernel corn,
  drained
2 tablespoons chopped
  green pepper
1/3 cup sour cream

1 tablespoon instant minced
  onion or ¼ cup chopped
3 drops hot pepper sauce
1 (8-ounce) can crescent
  dinner rolls
1 egg, slightly beaten
1 tablespoon sesame seeds

Heat oven to 350 degrees. In small bowl, combine cheese, corn, green pepper, sour cream, onion, and hot pepper sauce. Unroll dough into 2 long rectangles. Place on ungreased cookie sheet with long sides overlapping ½ inch; firmly press edges and perforations to seal. Press or roll to form 13x7-inch rectangle. Spread corn mixture in 2-inch strip lenghtwise down center of dough. Make 6 cuts, approximately 2 inches apart, on each side of rectangle just to edge of filling. To give braided appearance, fold strips of dough at an angle halfway across filling, alternating from side to side. Fold ends under to seal. Brush with beaten egg; sprinkle with sesame seed.

Bake 15-23 minutes or until golden brown. Slice and serve hot. Great! Serves 8.

GRASSHOPPER CHEESECAKE

1½ cups chocolate wafer
  crumbs (about 26 wafers)
¼ cup butter or oleo, melted
3 (8-ounce) packages cream
  cheese, softened
1½ cups sugar
4 eggs

¼ cup plus 2 tablespoons
  creme de menthe
3 tablespoons white creme
  de cacao
4 (1-ounce) squares semisweet
  chocolate
½ cup sour cream

Combine chocolate wafer crumbs and butter, stirring well. Press onto bottom of a 9-inch springform pan; set aside.

Beat cream cheese at medium speed of electric mixer until light and fluffy. Gradually add sugar, beating well. Add eggs, one at a time, beating well after each addition. Add egg yolk and beat well. Stir liqueurs into cream cheese mixture; spoon into crust. Bake at 350 degrees 55-60 minutes or until set. Cool thoroughly.

Melt chocolate in top of double boiler and allow to cool; stir in sour cream. Spread chocolate mixture over top of cheesecake. Chill well before serving.

CHERRY PINEAPPLE DESSERT CREPES

12 dessert crepes
1 (3-ounce) package cream
　cheese, softened
2/3 cup sour cream
¼ cup brown sugar
1 teaspoon lemon juice

1 (21-ounce) can cherry pie
　filling
1 (8-ounce) can crushed
　pineapple
¼ cup chopped pecans

Blend cream cheese, sour cream and brown sugar till smooth. Spoon a generous tablespoonful down center of each crepe; roll up. Place seam up on a lightly buttered cookie sheet. Bake 5 minutes at 350 degrees. (Or assemble in advance; cover and refrigerate until ready to bake--add 3 minutes to baking time.)

Meanwhile combine lemon juice, pie filling, and pineapple in a saucepan; heat through. To serve, place two warm crepe rolls on each dessert plate; spoon cherry-pineapple sauce over top; sprinkle with pecans and serve immediately. Serves 6.

Add flair to this dessert spectacular by heating the sauce in a chafing dish and spooning it over crepes at the table.

DESSERT CREPE BATTER:
3 eggs
½ cup milk
½ cup water
3 tablespoons melted butter

1 cup flour
1-2 tablespoons sugar
¼ teaspoon salt

Blend all ingredients one minute. Scrape sides of blender and blend again till smooth.

CHEESE BLINTZES

12 (6½-7-inch) dessert
　crepes
1 cup small curd cottage
　cheese
1 (3-ounce) package cream
　cheese, softened

¼ cup sugar
1 teaspoon vanilla
½ teaspoon grated orange or
　lemon peel
2 tablespoons butter
Sour cream

In small bowl, combine cottage and cream cheese, sugar, vanilla and peel; mix well. Spoon about 2 tablespoons cheese mixture into center of browned side of crepe. Fold one side over filling; fold opposite side over filling; bring one open end to center, then other open end. Cover and chill until serving time.

In skillet or chafing dish, melt butter, add blintzes seam side down and cook until browned. Turn and cook on other side until golden brown. Serve topped with sour cream.

CHEESE FACTS

CHEESE BOARD

A basic cheese board should have three cheeses: one zesty, one medium and one mild. Examples:

  Zesty: Sharp-aged Cheddar, Roquefort or Danish Bleu
Medium: Jarlsberg or Swiss, Camembert or Brie, Boursin
   Mild: Muenster or Havarti, Gouda or Edam

CHEESE UTENSILS

A cheese shaver or thin-bladed knife may be used for semi-firm cheeses such as Cheddar. Cheese boards with hinged wire cutters are also suitable. A forked-tip knife works well with semi-firm cheeses such as Gouda or Edam, and the tip is used to lift cheese to cracker or a dish. A butter knife may be used for soft cheeses.

DIET TIPS

To get the flavor of cream cheese with fewer calories, use Neufchatel.

Use raw vegetables (celery, cucumbers, broccoli, carrots, cauliflower) instead of crackers with your dips or cheese balls.

Read the label—cheeses made from skim milk or part-skim milk are lower in fat content and, therefore, lower in calories than those made from whole milk.

Use low fat cottage cheese instead of whole milk ricotta in your recipes.

CHEESE SUBSTITUTIONS

Generally it is safe to substitute and exchange cheeses with similar textures and flavors. A few suggestions follow.

CHEDDAR	Colby, Edam, Coon, Process American, Gouda
SWISS	Jarlsberg, Gruyere
MUENSTER	Monterey Jack, Brick, Bel Paese, Bonbel, Cream Havarti, Port du Salut
CREAM	Neufchatel
COTTAGE	Ricotta, Pot, Farmer
MOZZARELLA	Muenster, Bel Paese, domestic Swiss, Monterey Jack
PARMESAN	Romano, Provolone
BLEU	Roquefort

When making a substitution in a recipe, consider how the substitution might affect the flavor and texture of the dish. Be especially careful with the blue-veined cheeses; their flavors become even more distinct when cooked.

CHEESE AND FRUIT CHART

Here are some great tasting cheese and fruit combinations that make for a cool, light dessert or snack. Low on starch and full of nutrition, cheese and fruit is a delicious treat.

BLEU - Apples, pears

BRICK - Apples, cherries, grapes, honeydew melon, nectarines, pears, plums, strawberries

BRIE/CAMEMBERT - Apples, grapes, peaches, pears, plums

CHEDDAR - Apples, cherries, melon, pears

EDAM/GOUDA - Apples, grapes, oranges, pineapple, nectarines, plums

GOURMANDISE - Strawberries, cherries

MUENSTER - Apples, cantaloupe, cherries, grapes, honeydew melon, plums

PROVOLONE - Apples, pears

SWISS - Apples, green grapes, oranges, peaches, pineapple, melon

CHEESE SELECTION GUIDE

CHEESE	USES	ACCOMPANIMENTS	SUGGESTED WINES
Bel Paese (Italy, U.S.)	Dessert	Fresh fruit, Triscuits, pumpernickel, French or Italian whole wheat	Heavy white, full-bodied red
Bleu (France)	Dessert, dips, salads, appetizers, cheese trays	Fresh fruit, bland crackers	Full-bodied, assertive red
Bonbel (France)	Dessert	Fresh fruit, French or Italian rye, whole wheat	Semi-sweet sparkling wine
Brie (France)	Dessert	Fresh fruit, especially pears	Full-bodied red, fruity, white
Brick (U.S.)	Sandwiches, appetizers, cheese trays	Fresh fruit, bland crackers	Rose, semi-dry, white, beer
Camembert (France)	Dessert	Especially good with apples, strawberries	All reds, most whites
Cheddar (England, U.S.)	Dessert, cooking, sandwiches, salads, appetizers, cheese trays	Especially good with apples, pears	Sharp - Full-bodied reds, Mild - Rose
Colby (U.S.)	Cooking, appetizers	Crackers, fresh fruit	See Cheddar
Coon (U.S.)	Cooking, appetizers	Crackers, fresh fruit	Most reds
Cottage Cheese (U.S.)	Fruit salads, cooking, appetizers	Canned or fresh fruit	
Cream cheese (U.S.)	Dessert, sandwiches, salads, cooking	Jelly and crackers	
Edam (Holland)	Dessert, appetizers, cheese tray	Fresh fruit, whole wheat, Italian rye, French bread	Dry red
Emmenthal (Switzerland)	Cooking, appetizers	Fondue, crackers, plain slices, salt and peppered	Most whites
Feta (Greece)	Cooking, salads	Usually Greek salad	Light red, fruity white
Gouda (Holland)	Dessert, appetizers, cheese trays	Fresh fruit, crackers	Dry red
Gruyere (Switzerland)	Dessert, appetizers, fondue	Fresh fruit, Triscuits, rye bread	Mostly dry to semi-sweet whites
Jarlsberg (Norway)	Appetizers, desserts	Crackers, fruit	All wines, especially reds
Liederkranz (U.S.)	Appetizers, desserts	Crackers, bananas, pears, apples	Beer, most reds, especially burgundy
Limburger (Belgium)	Dessert	Fresh fruit, dark bread, bland crackers	Beer, most assertive red
Longhorn (U.S.)	Cooking, appetizers	Crackers, fresh fruit	See Cheddar
Monterey Jack (U.S.)	Cooking	Mexican dishes	All wines, especially rose or light red
Mozzarella (Italy)	Cooking, pizza	Italian foods	Dry red, dry white
Muenster	Sandwiches, cheese trays	Crackers, bread, nuts	Rose, light dry white
Parmesan (Italy)	Cooking, pizza	Italian foods	Dry red
Port Salut (France)	Dessert, appetizers, cheese trays	Fresh fruit, especially apples, crackers	Fruity white
Provolone (Italy)	Appetizers, cooking	Italian foods, stuffed olives	Full-bodied red
Ricotta (Italy)	Appetizers, cooking,	Fresh or canned fruit	
Romano (Italy)	Cooking	Italian foods	
Roquefort (France)	Dips, salads, appetizers, desserts	Bland crackers, fresh fruit, Tokay grapes	Full-bodied, assertive red
Swiss (Switzerland)	Cooking, salads, sandwiches, appetizers, Desserts, cheese trays	Fresh fruit, squares of crusty French bread	Most whites

INDEX

APPETIZERS

Artichoke Squares 38
Asparagus Roll-Ups 15
Bacon-Onion Cheese Log 33
Baked Chicken Nuggets 38
Camembert A La Ritz 50
Carol's Special Stuffed Celery 32
Caviar Cream Supreme 62
Cheese and Fruit Centerpiece 32
Cheese Cracker Crispies 56
Cheese Truffles 50
Cocktail Cheese Pastries 37
Creamy Shrimp Dip 34
Easy Cheesy Cocktail Suggestions 40
Fried Cheese 37
Gouda Wellington 39
Havarti Party Dip 33
Homemade Boursin 36
Hot Artichoke Dip 13
Hot Buttered Brie 50
Hot Chipped Beef Dip 13
Martha's Cheese Straws 55
Marvelous Seafood Mornay 35
Mexically Roll 33
Mozzarella Sticks 43
Nutty Bleu Chicken Log 33
Pepperoni 'N Cheese Crescents 13
Pineapple Cheese Ball 35
Pineapple Cheese Sculpture 34
Porcupine Ball 62
Ranch Cheese Mousse 38
Salmon Supreme 35
Sausage/Cheese Balls 39
Sesame Cheese Straws 55
Smokehouse Shrimp Ball 33
Spinach-Filled Cheese Pastries 37
Stuffed Mushrooms 14

BREAKFASTS AND BRUNCHES

Apple Cream Cheese Coffee Cake 52
Apricot Nibble Bread 54
Asparagus Roll-Ups 15
Bagel Breakfast Treat 8
Bee My Honey French Toast 8
Breakfast Sausage Apple Pie 9
Coffee Lover's Omelette 8
Colonial Breakfast 8
Delicious Brunch Pie 22
Easter Morning Coffee Cake 52
Eggs Gruyere For Two 8
Eggs Parmigiana 9
Golden Cheese Braid 72
Gouda Eggs 8
Hidden Delight Muffins 53
Nancy's Cheesy Waffles 22
Parmesan Pull-Apart Bread 67
Polka Dot Danish Rolls 53
Speedy Micro Breakfast 9
Sunrise Surprise 9

BREADS

Apple Cream Cheese Coffee Cake 52
Apricot Nibble Bread 54
Bishop's Swiss Beer Bread 56
Cheese Dough 54
Cheese Popover Puffs 29
Cheesy Buns 57
Cocktail Cheese Pastries 37
Country Cheese Corn Bread 28
Dilly-licious Bread 58
Easter Morning Coffee Cake 52
Golden Cheese Braid 72
Good-For-the-Soul Cheese Bread 57
Hidden Delight Muffins 53
Italian Mozzarella Loaf 43
Little Cheese Puffs 48
Mozzarella Sticks 43
Pepperoni 'N Cheese Crescents 13
Polka Dot Danish Rolls 53
Silo Bread 29
Tipsy Bread 55

CAKES, PIES, DESSERTS

Brandy Alexandria Souffle 20
Carol's Cherry Cheesecake 30
Cheddar Cheese Pie 30
Cheesapple Dumplings 54
Cheese Blintzes 73
Cheese Popover Puffs 29
Cherry Pineapple Dessert Crepes 73
Cream Cheese Frosting 60
Frozen Peanut Butter Pie 30
Grasshopper Cheesecake 72
Heavenly Kahlua Cheesecake 49
Little Cheese Puffs 48
Mint Chocolate Parfait Pie 20
Minted Brownies 59
Mystery Pecan Pie 60
Parish Pecan Pound Cake 60

Sunshine Bars 59
Tiny Heavenly Cheesecakes 39

CASSEROLES, SOUFFLES, QUICHES

Almond Fettuccine 44
Barn Dance Dish 24
Boursin Cheese Quiche 44
Broccoli 'N Rice 'R Nice 68
Cheesy Potato Casserole 15
Chili Corn Casserole 45
Country Corn Pudding 26
Easy Souffle 15
Eggplant Provolone 27
Fettuccine Magnifico 69
Fluffy Potato Casserole 24
Grecian One-Dish Meal 45
Harry's Favorite Casserole 17
Heavenly Potato Clouds 66
Italian Parcheesi Pasta 18
La Bella Lasagna 47
Meatless Cottage Cheese Meatloaf 28
Mexican Cheese Casserole 48
Muenstrously Delicious Onion Casserole 26
Ole! Rice Casserole 17
Old-Fashioned Macaroni and Cheese Bake 26
Parmesan Cheese Souffle 25
Quiche Lorraine 44
Savory Mashed Potato Casserole 17
Seashell-Provolone Casserole 71
Suppertime Celery 28
Swiss Lima Casserole 24
Zucchini Zelicious 16

EGGS

Coffee Lover's Omelette 8
Eggs Gruyere For Two 8
Eggs Parmiagiana 9
Gouda Eggs 8
Speedy Micro Breakfast 9

FRUIT

Ambrosia Cream Salad 64
Apple Cream Cheese Coffee Cake 52
Breakfast Sausage Apple Pie 9
Cheesapple Dumplings 54
Cheese and Fruit Centerpiece 32
Cherry Pineapple Dessert Crepes 73
Elegante Swiss Broccoli Soup 62

Fruit Salad with Cream Cheese Pearls 10
Pink Arctic Freeze 10
Rainbow Salad 10

MEATS

Beef Burgundy Stroganoff 47
Breakfast Sausage Apple Pie 9
Crusty Taco Squares 46
Hot Chipped Beef Dip 13
Hot Turkey Cheesewiches 11
Italian Parcheesi Pasta 18
Italian Sausage Pizza 46
Jim's Jelly-Roll Meatloaf 70
La Bella Lasagna 47
Mama Mia Meatloaf 19
Nacho Taco Salad 42
Pepperoni 'N Cheese Crescents 13
Piedmont Veal Cutlets 47
Quiche Lorraine 44
Sausage/Cheese Balls 39
Seashell-Provolone Casserole 71
Speedy Micro Breakfast (ham) 9
Sunrise Surprise (ham) 9
Swiss Reuben Pie 70

MICROWAVE

Brandy Alexander Souffle 20
Chicken Ala Romano 18
Delicate French Onion Soup 12
Hot Artichoke Dip 13
Hot Chipped Beef Dip 13
Hot Turkey Cheesewiches 11
Italian Parcheesi Pasta 18
Mama Mia Meatloaf 19
Microwave Cheese Sauce 14
Microwave Zucchini Mozzarella 45
Open Face Havarti Cheesewich 11
Quick-Fix Parmesan Fish 19
Savory Mashed Potato Casserole 17
Speedy Micro Breakfast 9
Spinach Larraine 16
Stuffed Mushrooms 14
Zucchini Zelicious 16

POULTRY AND SEAFOOD

Bagel Breakfast Treat (salmon) 8
Baked Chicken Nuggets 38
Chicken Ala Romano 18
Chicken Parmicheesa 71

Cool Shrimp Dip 34
Festive Chicken With Asparagus 69
Hot Crabmeat Spread 36
Marvelous Seafood Mornay 35
Quick-Fix Parmesan Fish 19
Salmon Supreme 35

SALADS

Acropolis Salad 42
Ambrosia Cream Salad 64
Cheesy Tato Salad 10
Chef's Three-Cheese Salad 63
Country Slaw 23
English Pea 'N Cheddar Cheese
  Salad 65
Farmer's Garden Salad 23
Fruit Salad with Cream Cheese
  Pearls 10
Nacho Taco Salad 42
Pink Arctic Freeze 10
Rainbow Salad 10
Red River Mountain Salad 10
Tomato Aspic with Bleu Cheese
  Topping 65

SALAD DRESSINGS

Bleu Cheese Topping 65
Cheese Bacon Dressing 64
Chef's Dressing 63
Greek Dressing 42
Romano Salad Dressing 42
Roquefort Cheese Dressing 64
Southern Roquefort Cheese
  Dressing 64

SANDWICHES

Grilled Muenster Cheesewich 11
Hot Turkey Cheesewiches 11
Mozzarella Sticks 43
Open Face Havarti Cheesewich 11
Perfect Pimento Spread 36

SAUCES AND SPREADS

Artichoke Spread 36
Basic White Sauce 28
Bleu Cheese Sauce 14
Cheddar Butter Spread 11
Hot Crabmeat Spread 36
Microwave Cheese Sauce 14
Perfect Pimento Spread 36
Ranch Cheese Mousse 38

SOUPS

Down Home Cheddar Cheese
  Soup 23
Edam Up Soup 63
Elegante Swiss Broccoli Soup 62
Delicate French Onion Soup 12
Popcorn Soup 12
Rinktum Diddy 23

VEGETABLES

Artichoke Spread 36
Artichoke Squares 38
Asparagus Roll-Ups 15
Baked Potato Boats 27
Barn Dance Dish 24
Broccoli 'N Rice 'R Nice 68
Broiled Parmesan Tomatoes 16
Carol's Special Stuffed Celery 32
Carrots Au Gratin 66
Cheeseasy Cauliflower 25
Cheesy Potato Casserole 15
Cheesy Tato Salad 10
Chili Corn Casserole 45
Country Corn Pudding 26
Country Slaw 23
Delicate Swiss Cheese Grits 67
Delicious Brunch Pie 22
Eggplant Provolone 27
English Pea 'N Cheddar Cheese
  Salad 65
Fancy French Green Beans 67
Farmer's Garden Salad 23
Fluffy Potato Casserole 24
Grecian One-Dish Meal 45
Heavenly Potato Clouds 66
Microwave Garlic Cheese Grits 66
Microwave Zucchini Mozzarella 45
Muenstrously Delicious Onion
  Casserole 26
Ole! Rice Casserole 17
Savory Mashed Potato Casserole 17
Spicy Spinach-Stuffed Squash 68
Spinach Elegante 65
Spinach-Filled Cheese Pastries 37
Spinach Larraine 16
Spinach with Cream Cheese 25
Stuffed Mushrooms 14
Suppertime Celery 28
Swiss Lima Casserole 24
Zucchini-Tomato Pie 27
Zucchini Zelicious 16

The Quail Ridge Press Cookbook Series:

THE COUNTRY MOUSE $4.95
ANY TIME'S A PARTY! $4.95
THE TWELVE DAYS OF CHRISTMAS COOKBOOK $4.95
THE SEVEN CHOCOLATE SINS $4.95
A SALAD A DAY $4.95
QUICKIES FOR SINGLES $4.95
HORS D'OEUVRES EVERYBODY LOVES $4.95
BEST OF THE BEST FROM MISSISSIPPI $9.95
BEST OF THE BEST FROM LOUISIANA $11.95

If these books are not available from a local merchant, they may be ordered directly from:

QUAIL RIDGE PRESS
P. O. Box 123
Brandon, MS 39042

Mississippi residents add 6% sales tax.